Health-Care Reform

A Surgeon's Perspective

Ashraf A. Hilmy,
MD, MBA, FACS, FACHE

iUniverse, Inc.
Bloomington

Health-Care Reform
A Surgeon's Perspective

Copyright © 2012 by Ashraf A Hilmy, MD, MBA, FACS, FACHE

All rights reserved. No part of this book may be used or reproduced by any means, graphic, electronic, or mechanical, including photocopying, recording, taping or by any information storage retrieval system without the written permission of the publisher except in the case of brief quotations embodied in critical articles and reviews.

iUniverse books may be ordered through booksellers or by contacting:

iUniverse
1663 Liberty Drive
Bloomington, IN 47403
www.iuniverse.com
1-800-Authors (1-800-288-4677)

Because of the dynamic nature of the Internet, any web addresses or links contained in this book may have changed since publication and may no longer be valid. The views expressed in this work are solely those of the author and do not necessarily reflect the views of the publisher, and the publisher hereby disclaims any responsibility for them.

Any people depicted in stock imagery provided by Thinkstock are models, and such images are being used for illustrative purposes only.

Certain stock imagery © Thinkstock.

ISBN: 978-1-4759-5230-8 (sc)
ISBN: 978-1-4759-5229-2 (hc)
ISBN: 978-1-4759-5231-5 (e)

Library of Congress Control Number: 2012917892

Printed in the United States of America

iUniverse rev. date: 10/29/2012

Contents

Introduction	vii
Chapter 1: Health-Care Delivery in the United States	1
Chapter 2: Comparative Health-Care Delivery Model Analysis	11
Chapter 3: Drivers of Health-Care Costs	19
Chapter 4: Specific Examples of Anonymous Cases	39
Chapter 5: Meaningful Reform	57
Chapter 6: Postscript/Obamacare	95
Conclusion	99
Bibliography	101

Introduction

Ryan, a twenty-four-year-old married man with one child, was employed by a pest control company and came to my office with a huge recurrent right groin hernia. He'd had a previous repair done elsewhere about four years prior. The hernia had become increasingly bothersome. It was causing him quite a bit of pain and eventually interfered with his ability to perform his job. He had a very noticeable bulge in the right groin extending down to his scrotum, and he had to conceal the bulge with loose-fitting clothing.

This man desperately needed a second hernia repair surgery. The hernia was painful, interfering with his ability to work, and it was potentially life threatening because the herniated intestines could become strangulated and result in gangrene of the intestines. There was just one problem: he did not have health insurance. His employer did not offer it, and he could not afford it on his meager salary. His financial obligations for the surgery would have been as follows: hospital fee $11,833, with a 40 percent discount if paid up front; anesthesia about $1,200; the surgery fee, which I discounted to $610; and a few other incidental charges that usually show up. The grand total was $13,693. Ryan could not afford this fee because his annual salary was $15,600 when he was working full-time. He had to cut back to part-time employment because of his increasingly symptomatic hernia and was making only about $200 a month.

Ryan sought assistance from Medicaid, which is a federal program created to fund health-care costs of economically challenged individuals. He was turned down! The reason given was that he was employed, had a late-model car, and had a life insurance policy! Next Ryan went to the

Rio Grande Valley Indigent Care Program, which, as the name implies, is set up to assist indigent people. He was turned down for the same reasons! His next step was DARS, the Department of Assistive and Rehabilitative Services. This is a federal program designed to assist low-income working people or hospital-based assistance programs that are usually federal or grant funded. Once again, Ryan did not qualify. All of these resources are hit-and-miss programs that haven't always come through for my patients.

This productive member of our society was unable to continue his meager but gainful employment and was unable to get assistance to take care of his medical condition so he could return to gainful employment. Something is very, very wrong with this picture.

Here is another example of our broken system, with emphasis on the other end of the spectrum. My patient Norma is a thirty-seven-year-old female who had a breast problem. She had an abnormal mammogram and an abnormal breast ultrasound study. Her risk factors for breast cancer were relatively low, and the breast imaging studies were not conclusive for breast cancer. Further options included repeating the breast imaging with a mammogram and ultrasound in six months, a breast biopsy, or proceeding with an MRI (magnetic resonance imaging) of the breast. MRI is a much more sensitive study for detecting early breast cancer, but it is also much more expensive.

I advised Norma that my index of concern for breast cancer was relatively low. I did not feel she was a good candidate for biopsy because of certain features on the mammogram and ultrasound and because of my low index of suspicion. Norma had some concerns about the abnormal breast imaging and wanted further reassurance. We opted for an MRI as the best option since it was noninvasive and highly sensitive. I ordered it and set up a follow-up appointment.

Her insurance company declined to cover the expense, stating that it was not indicated, and kicked up the request to the company's in-house physician for his review. A couple of days later, I received a phone call from said physician for a peer-to-peer review of the case. After I presented her case and answered his questions, the company physician informed me that the MRI was not indicated but would be covered anyway.

I didn't understand what he had just said. "Excuse me," I said, "how can you authorize an MRI if you say it's not indicated?" The doctor understood my surprise and didn't expect me to understand, but then

Health-Care Reform: A Surgeon's Perspective

he informed me that he could not decline to cover the procedure because her husband was a federal employee and she had federal insurance. Therefore, he was obliged to allow it! Had she not had federal insurance, he would have turned her down. No discrimination here!

These two opening vignettes help shed some light on how our health-care delivery system is flawed and the fact that it needs serious reform. As you read on in this book, you'll find no political correctness, only honest, insightful debate that is based on experience and opinions collected with surgical precision during my over-thirty-year career in the practice of medicine. As a small business owner of my surgical practice of general, vascular, advanced laparoscopic, robotic, and cosmetic surgery in south Texas; an assistant professor of surgery teaching medical students and residents; and a holder of an MBA with an emphasis on health care, I have the real life and academic experience to digest the complexities of health-care delivery in the United States.

I have practiced in solo practice, partnership practice, and large group practice settings and have experienced salaried employment and private fees for service reimbursement. I have done my undergraduate schooling in India, medical school and internship in Egypt, and postgraduate training in medicine, anesthesia, cardiac anesthesia, and surgery in the United States. I have achieved board certification in health-care administration, surgery, anesthesia, and critical-care medicine and am a fellow of the American College of Surgeons and the American College of Healthcare Executives. I have also practiced surgery, anesthesia, critical-care medicine, and emergency medicine at various hospitals across the country.

I have held several executive positions at various hospitals (chief of surgery, chief of staff, medical director for bariatric surgery, director of neuroanesthesia, and business consultant for surgical growth), which has given me the opportunity to view health-care delivery from a different perspective. These hospitals have ranged in nature and size from small and medium community hospitals to large academic tertiary care institutions and also have varied geographically across the United States.

Hailing from Egypt and having lived in and traveled to various countries in the world (the United States, Canada, Mexico, Holland, India, England, Spain, France, Greece, Italy, Costa Rica, Panama, Nicaragua, Iraq, Syria, Kuwait, Lebanon, New Zealand, and Australia, to name a few), I have had the opportunity to experience different health-care delivery models at work. Though none are perfect, there are much better models out there than what the United States has to offer.

In this book, I set out first to describe the current health-care system, discuss its flaws, and compare it to other world models. I will also explain the drivers of health-care costs and offer specific anonymous case examples of inefficient, expensive medicine being practiced that I have encountered in my personal experience so you will be able to see these cost drivers at work in clinical medicine. Finally, I will provide constructive criticism of health-care delivery in the United States and propose solutions to the problem of health-care reform.

No significant major change is done without some sacrifice. Sacrifice will overlap many different aspects of the current health-care delivery paradigm, some with serious societal implications, but as the old saying goes, "You can't have your cake and eat it too." Something has to give. Read on with an open mind, and see for yourself how I will expose the drivers of health-care costs and what we need to do as a nation to put the brakes on unparalleled escalation in health-care expenditures.

Remember, I am a surgeon. I will not sugarcoat it or beat around the bush. I will tell it as it is with surgical precision. Some of my readers will not agree, and some (medical colleagues, lawyers, administrators, and citizens alike) will be offended as I put a portion of the blame squarely upon their shoulders, but so be it.

As I said, there will be no political correctness here. I have a message to deliver, and deliver it I will. I make no apologies. I am just reporting facts and personal opinion. I am not setting out to intentionally hurt anyone, but people will be hurt as I tackle different cost drivers. To accomplish the task of this book—namely, to discuss meaningful health-care reform—I cannot be politically correct because this will only kick the can further down the road and hide the problems under the rug for fear of offending someone. We have had enough of that nonsense already! We must put each and every problem under the spotlight and scrutinize it relentlessly until we have found a solution. We need to be honest and open-minded about this debate if we are ever going to accomplish any meaningful changes.

I can tell you with certainty that a two-thousand-plus-page document is not required to fix health care. Anything that complicated is full of quagmire and bureaucracy that has been generated by government officials who have no clue as to how health care really works. Even the Supreme Court justices haven't been able to read this document in its entirety. You need the front-line people who are in the business of health-care delivery day in and day out to address the issues they know intimately. Those on the front lines need the freedom to tackle the problems head on, with decisive, constructive, meaningful criticism and reform.

And finally, to satisfy the lawyers and my editor, as silly as it might seem, I am advised to state a medical disclaimer that any medical discussions in this book are used to display specific case examples of how certain actions increase the cost of health care and are not intended as advice. These examples should not lead the reader to take health-care actions based on these discussions.

Chapter 1:
Health-Care Delivery in the United States

About half of the health care delivered in the United States is done by private, physician-owned practices, down from 70 percent in 2002 to 50 percent in 2008.[1] This statistic does not differentiate between independent hospitals hiring physicians and integrated health-care systems hiring physicians. It also does not differentiate between physicians employed by the government (Veterans Administration, National Health Service) and large, integrated health-care systems. Indeed, the overall number of employed physicians is increasing and is projected to grow by 24 percent between 2010 and 2020, according to the Bureau of Labor Statistics.[2]

But that does not mean that they are being employed by large, integrated multispecialty group practice organizations such as the Mayo Clinic. These statistics pool all employed physicians into one big pot. There is a big difference between being employed by a stand-alone hospital as a hospitalist (a primary care physician who practices at the hospital without an outpatient practice) and being employed by a large, integrated, multispecialty health-care system. Though the physician is employed, and thus will be a statistical number adding to the pool of employed physicians, that employment model does not offer the advantages of a comprehensive health-care system, as will be illustrated.

---

1   http://www.nejm.org/doi/full/10.1056/NEJMp1101959.

2   http://www.bls.gov/ooh/Healthcare/Physicians-and-surgeons.htm.

With the exception of a few large multispecialty group practices—Mayo Clinic, Scott and White, Kaiser Permanente, and Marshfield Clinic, to name a few—the majority of health care is delivered through small, mom-and-pop or cottage industry practices on a fee-for-service basis. The introduction of the group practice model occurred around the turn of the twentieth century. It was pioneered by the Mayo brothers in Minnesota and by Garfield and Kaiser around the Great Depression at a time when that concept was unheard of.

Under the current model, payment flows from the payer source—private insurance, Medicaid, Medicare, and private pay—separately to providers, which include hospitals, medical practices, and ancillary providers (labs, outside radiology centers, etc.). There is no integration of services or resources between these providers. It's a free-for-all model with everyone billing separately for their services (fee-for-service).

The cottage industry model consists of multiple independent practices—family practice, internal medicine, surgeon, cardiologist, gastroenterologist, etc.—that are all geographically and otherwise independent of each other. Each practice has its own record keeping. Some have paper charts and others electronic medical records of varying types that do not communicate with each other or with hospital medical records. Without the pooling of resources, the cost of advanced information technology that would allow for all physicians to have access to a common electronic medical record is out of reach. Consequently, each practitioner does not have immediate access to information contained in other medical records. Each practice has its own billing and administrative staff, all of which could be pooled together to serve a larger group practice for a fraction of the cost.

There isn't an overseeing body that could implement best-practice guidelines and insist on evidence-based medicine as the gold standard to be emulated. Each practitioner is independent and answers to no one. There is no accountability because there isn't a physician employer. There is no group organizational culture. There is also no economic credentialing. For example, when comparing the cost of health-care delivery among different physicians for similar outcomes, if it costs the system twice as much for me to remove an appendix than it does my colleague and the outcomes are similar, then I'm costing the system too much money compared to my colleague, and I should be counseled accordingly.

At the end of the day, the cottage-industry physician answers to no one. He is not held accountable for the cost of care that is being delivered or for the best practice guidelines that are to be emulated. His compensation is dependent upon how many procedures he does. His financial rapport with his colleagues depends upon referring patients to them for further testing, and the "scratch my back, I'll scratch yours" principle takes hold. Also consider this in light of the "cover my ass" medicine that is practiced in fear of medico-legal retribution. Everyone is scared of being sued, so many times multiple experts are called in to manage cases. There is an old saying in medicine: "It is easier for six people to carry the coffin."

> **What Is the Cottage Industry?**
>
> Common characteristics of cottage industry medical practices:
>
> - Multiple independent practices
> - In economic competition
> - No cost or resource sharing
> - No common patient record
> - No financial incentive to curtail services
> - More done = more money
> - No allegiance to a hospital
> - Limited resources for IT/EMR
> - No requirement for EBM or quality activities
>
> IT= information technology
>
> EMR= electronic medical record
>
> EBM= evidence-based medicine

In cottage-industry medicine, physicians have no allegiance to any particular hospital, laboratory, or imaging center, so patients are sent to various facilities for fragmented portions of their care depending on the preference of the treating physician. There is no pooling of resources, so each medical encounter is a new one for the patient. There is no common medical record, so needless documents are generated and regenerated. Diagnostic tests are repeated over and over at the discretion of the treating physician. There is no medical home for the patient.

Frank, a sixty-seven-year-old man with a history of diabetes, high blood pressure, and heart failure, presents to the emergency department of hospital X at 10:00 p.m. with complaints of abdominal pain, nausea, and vomiting. The emergency medicine doctor on duty evaluates the patient. A decision is made that the patient needs to be admitted to the hospital for further evaluation and treatment of his abdominal pain, which is believed due to acute cholecystitis—an inflammation of the gall bladder—and for management of his diabetes and heart failure, both of which are out of control.

Frank's primary medical provider does not practice at hospital X and so does not come to take care of Frank's medical needs. The emergency department does not have access to Frank's medical records from his primary provider. There is no way to know what has been done for Frank's diabetes and heart failure, like what medicines he has been given, what tests have been done, and what treatment strategies have been implemented. Similarly, the treating physician does not have access to the evaluation that was done for Frank at another hospital, hospital Y, a couple of days earlier for the same complaints.

Another barrage of tests is ordered—blood work, an echocardiogram, a CAT scan of the abdomen, and an abdominal ultrasound, all of which have been done at another facility just days before. The same conclusion is reached: Frank has a bad gall bladder that needs to be surgically removed. The previous hospital evaluation led to a recommendation that Frank should follow up with a surgeon for a cholecystectomy—an operation to remove his gall bladder. Frank needed a referral from his primary doctor to see a surgeon, and his primary physician made an appointment for him a week later, but his symptoms increased, prompting his visit to the emergency department. Though his doctor referred him to hospital Y, Frank preferred hospital X because it was closer to his home and had a friendlier staff.

So Frank is admitted to hospital X, where a team of the hospital's doctors—internal medicine doctors who limit their practice to the hospital setting—a surgeon, and a cardiologist are caring for Frank. He is medically optimized and undergoes a cholecystectomy. His medications are adjusted to manage his diabetes and his heart failure, and he is discharged home. The medical doctors who adjusted his medications do not have any follow-up arrangements for Frank because they are not his primary care team, and his primary doctor has no idea that his medications have been changed.

Frank is confused by his new medication schedule because it conflicts with what his doctor had prescribed, so he doesn't stick to the schedule that was arranged for him at the hospital. Within a week, he is readmitted to the hospital with worsening heart failure. Though Frank's case is fictional, used it to display the shortcomings of our system, it is historical fiction that I have conjured from multiple similar cases from my practice. This really happens day in and day out.

There is absolutely no incentive for physicians to limit the cost of patient encounters. In fact, it is quite the contrary. A physician is financially rewarded for doing more. That is how the fee-for-service reimbursement system works. A doctor is compensated based on the number of encounters, the complexity of the encounter, and the interventions done. As Atul Gawande pointed out in his 2009 *New Yorker* article, "The Cost Conundrum" (Gawande, 2009), patients are ATM machines for doctors. They are passed on from one practitioner to the next, and all the practitioners do countless procedures in a fee-for-service model with no accountability whatsoever.

According to the Center for Medicaid and Medicare Services, there is tremendous variability in the cost of delivering health care. Medicare expenditures per enrolled patient in Miami, Florida, are twice the amount spent in Minneapolis, Minnesota, for similar patients (*Dartmouth Atlas of Health Care*, 2012). There is no economic credentialing or accountability.

There are numerous legal and societal pressures on physicians to do more and more. I can absolutely tell you without a fraction of a doubt that a large percentage of what we do is called "CYA"—cover your ass! With the current malpractice system, physicians are terrified of being sued. We order all sorts of unnecessary tests to make sure we don't miss that one-in-a-million chance of a rare disease or presentation to protect ourselves from malpractice attorneys. We provide services that most of the world would deem unnecessary. We have nursing home patients who are in their eighties and nineties in a vegetative state, with no meaningful quality of life, who are subjected to numerous interventions. There is no cost accountability for families because the family members are not financially responsible for the cost of health care delivered to Medicaid and Medicare recipients. The indigent family members of an eighty-nine-year-old, demented, vegetative state nursing home patient whose dialysis funding comes from Medicare have no financial obligation. They don't have a dog in the financial fight. They say, "Let's keep dialyzing Grandma; it's costing us nothing." I will get into cost drivers later in the book, but first I will give you an introduction to the practice of medicine in our country.

Let's begin by examining how we pay for health care in the United States. The payment pool is divided into private insurance, private pay (which is frequently equivalent to no pay) health maintenance organizations, and military insurance. In 2004, a study conducted by the US Department of Health and Human Services found that the sources of insurance coverage for the US population are distributed as follows: employer-provided (60 percent), Medicare (14 percent), and Medicaid/SCHIP (State Children's Health Insurance Program) (13 percent). Slightly smaller percentages are covered either by insurance purchased directly (9 percent) or military insurance (4 percent).[3] That leaves a remaining 16 percent of the total population—50 million Americans—who are classified as uninsured. So that means that the other 84 percent are fine and dandy, right? *Not!* Insurance premiums are outrageously high, so many people raise their deductibles to make their monthly payments more affordable. And let's not forget about the 20 percent co-pay on major medical expenses. Just because you have insurance doesn't mean you're off the hook.

Imagine that you are a gainfully employed father of three working for "the man." You live in the suburbs making a salary of $125,000 a year. Your oldest kid has a paper route, and your wife pulls in a cool $60,000 managing a medical practice. All of this makes you one of the lucky well-to-do employed Americans with a stable job and health insurance. Many people would love to have that kind of income and have insurance to boot.

Now let's say your luck happens to change, and you are afflicted with a form of leukemia! You are told that a bone marrow transplant is needed at a cost of $50,000 to $200,000.[4] That doesn't include the other hospital and doctors' bills on top of that. For starters, your out-of-pocket expenses are usually 20 percent of the total cost, and then you can look forward to the grind of spending thousands of dollars a month on maintenance meds (Erbitux, an anticancer drug, costs about $10,000 a month). Imagine that you are told all of this, only to learn that your insurance company will not cover you any longer because you have maxed out your lifetime benefit allowance. Things are not so rosy anymore, are they?

Actually, you are fine if you fall below the poverty line or are disabled because you automatically qualify for Medicaid or Medicare coverage. You can't get turned down by any emergency room, and you will have no worries about co-pays or deductibles because you will have no resources to pay for them, and your credit score will be the least of your worries.

---

3   http://aspe.hhs.gov/health/reports/05/uninsured-cps/index.htm#2.

4   http://www.nbmtlink.org/.

You're also fine if you're in the upper echelon of society and can afford insurance, deductibles, and co-pays.

According to a recent *Time Magazine* article, a Pew Research Center survey found that half of all Americans self-identify as middle class (Suddath, 2009). These are the folks who hurt—people who are employed in small businesses, teachers, and nurses. The cost of providing or supporting health insurance becomes prohibitive and cuts into the economic stability of the business or individual. This in turn cuts into consumers' discretionary income and decreases national economic activity.

According to studies, 13 to 17 percent of Americans (45 million) live below the US government's defined poverty line. Poverty is defined by the US Department of Health and Human Services (2011) as an annual household income below $22,350 for a family of four. According to the US Census Bureau, 40 percent of Americans will dip below the poverty line over a ten-year period, and 58 percent will spend one year living below the poverty line.

As a small business owner, I write off approximately 15 to 20 percent of my work as charity. I am obliged to care for uninsured patients who come into the hospital. I also care for private patients for humanitarian reasons. I am not about to turn away a patient with breast cancer because she or he can't afford my bill—and yes, breast cancer does occur in males.

I am forced to participate in Medicare's fee program if I want to be paid directly by Medicare. I can opt out of Medicare, which allows me to bill the patient directly at my nondiscounted fee. However, Medicare will pay the patient at their discounted fee, and then it's up to me to collect the the remaining fee from the patient. The majority of my Medicare patients are not sitting in a pretty place financially, so there is no guarantee the patient will actually pay my fee. As a result, it is much better for me to accept Medicare's rates and get paid directly by the government. This program means I cannot balance-bill patients for the difference between my fee schedule and Medicare's allowed charge.

For example, I may charge $3,000 to perform a gall bladder operation, but Medicare only allows $700, and Medicaid allows $560. I can opt out of the program, which means I can bill the patient directly for $3,000 and hope to get paid. The patient will submit paperwork to CMS (Centers for Medicare & Medicaid Services) and collect the allowable amount from CMS and owe me the balance. My other choice is to opt in, which allows me to bill CMS for the discounted amount, which will come straight to me. Similarly, insurance companies force physicians to accept a negotiated fee for their services so they can become preferred providers. Refusing to accept the negotiated fee results in physicans being classified as out-of-network, which places significant limitations on the eligible patient pool for that physician.

Actually, relative to inflation, Medicare's reimbursment has dropped about 25 percent over the last decade ending in 2008. I am earning 25 to 30 percent less for the same procedures that I do now than I did ten years ago! This steady drop in reimbursement, coupled with the increasing complexity of managing a medical practice, has taken its toll. More manpower hours are required as my office staff jump through hoops to deal with appeals for denials and more administrative bureaucracy than ever before. The cost and complexity of doing business continues to rise steadily as the rate of reimbursment by Medicare continues to drop for the same services. As a result, my fee schedule cannot even keep up with the consumer price index for health care.

Now consider a retail store (Dillards, for example) that has lost inventory in a warehouse fire or theft or has lost revenue to bad debt. According to accepted US accounting standards, the loss can be written off as a business loss or bad debt. This means that the company can deduct that amount off its total annual revenue so it will not be taxed.

Well, guess what? I can't do that. If I spend four hours operating in the middle of the night to save a patient involved in a car wreck or lose office productivity because I had to cancel my elective patients to take care of an uninsured patient with acute appendicitis, I can't write that loss off as bad debt. I also cannot write off any of the mandatory negotiated fee schedule variances between what is allowed and what I typically charge private-pay patients. All lost revenue to bad debt on insurance co-pays and deductibles is also out the window, and I cannot write it off as bad debt. This seems like a double standard, doesn't it? It is!

After all, we live by the golden rule: he who has the gold makes the rules! Well, doctors surely don't have the legislative gold; lawyers do. Lawyers make the rules. Lawyers comprise the backbone of American government. Doctors really don't have a say in government. The American Medical Association is rivaled by numerous other organizations with lobbying powers—the American Civil Liberties

Health-Care Reform: A Surgeon's Perspective

Union, chambers of commerce, the National Rifle Association, and the National Trial Lawyers Association, to cite a few. All of these may have more influence than the AMA because there are more vested interests politically holding hands with them than with the AMA.

Now let's examine US expenditures on health care compared to the gross domestic product (GDP) over the last few decades. According to the Congressional Budget Office, total spending on health services and supplies has risen from 4.7 percent of GDP in 1960 to 14.9 percent in 2005. Current spending is around 18 percent and is predicted to reach over 21 percent by 2020 (Davis, 2012). According to James Orlikoff,[5] health-care expenditure is growing at a rate that is two to six times the rate of economic expansion. Compare the percentage of GDP spent on health care to that spent on the military. It is 18 versus 5 percent, respectively! The fastest-growing expense for the pentagon is not military technology but health care! Similarly, the most expensive part of an American-made car is the cost of health care associated with manufacturing that car (health-care costs for workers) at $1,800 to $2,200 per car compared to Japan where the most expensive part of a Japanese car is the cost of steel. Orlikoff goes on to note that 30 percent of health-care expenditures in the United States add no clinical value to a patient's care. It is spent on such things as repeating labs already done because they are not available to the physician at the time of encounter, clerical work, such as refiling insurance claims after denial, and so on. This accounts for 5 percent of GDP. Furthermore, 4.4 million hospital admissions are preventable, accounting for thirty-one billion dollars of avoidable expenses.[6]

As I will demonstrate in a later chapter, we spend more on health care than any other westernized, easternized, or anyother "ized" country in the world and have less to show for it. The reasons for this will be explained later. I'm just trying to give you a taste of reality here.

Now, why is this so? As I said, a detailed analysis will follow, but as preview, let me say that good care costs money. Good care that is

---

[5] James Orlikoff is the president of Orlikoff and Associates, Inc., a consulting firm specializing in health-care governance and leadership, strategy, quality, and organizational development and is also the national advisor to the American Hospital Association and senior consultant to the Center for Health Care Governance.

[6] http://www.ghx.com/product-pages/industry-resources/blog-the-healthcare-hub/entryid/27.aspx, and personal communications.

delivered in an unaccountable manner costs more money. Good care that is delivered in an environment of fear of retribution costs even more money.

Chapter 2: Comparative Health-Care Delivery Model Analysis

On December 10, 1948, the General Assembly of the United Nations (third session) adopted the Universal Declaration of Human Rights (UDHR) as part of the International Bill of Human Rights (IBHR). The IBHR addresses the following:

- UDHR
- Right to petition
- Fate of minorities
- Publicity to be given to the UDHR
- Preparation of a draft covenant on human rights and draft measures of implementation

The resolution was adopted in response to the international social, political, economic, and humanitarian conditions that prevailed following World War II. The UDHR consists of thirty articles addressing a range of issues, which have been elaborated on in subsequent international treaties, regional human rights instruments, and national constitutions and laws. Article Twenty-Five specifically addresses health care:

> (1) Everyone has the right to a standard of living adequate for the health and well-being of himself and of his family, including food, clothing, housing, and medical care and necessary social

services, and the right to security in the event of unemployment, sickness, disability, widowhood, old age or other lack of livelihood in circumstances beyond his control.

(2) Motherhood and childhood are entitled to special care and assistance. All children, whether born in or out of wedlock, shall enjoy the same social protection.

Similarly the World Health Organization holds the following position:

Good health is essential to human welfare and to sustained economic and social development. WHO's Member States have set themselves the target of developing their health financing systems to ensure that all people can use health services, while being protected against financial hardship associated with paying for them. (World Health Organization, 2010)

Most current universal health-care systems were implemented in the period following the Second World War. In fact, every UN member nation signed and ratified the Universal Declaration of Human Rights, with the exception of the United States. The United States elected not to ratify the social and economic rights sections, including the right-to-health section outlined in Article Twenty-Five. Having taken this bold and in-your-face step, you'd think the United States would have something to show for it. The public is led to believe that health care in the United States is unrivaled. We believe that life expectancy, infant mortality, access to health care, and health-care expenditures as a percentage of GDP are the best in the world. If you believe this, I have news for you. Check out the following. Thirty-two of the thirty-three developed nations have universal health care, with the United States being the lone exception. The list of nations with universal health care includes Norway, which first adopted its health-care system in 1912.

Health-Care Reform: A Surgeon's Perspective

Nations with Universal Health Care		
Country	**Start Date of Universal Health Care**	**System Type**
Norway	1912	Single Payer
New Zealand	1938	Two Tier
Japan	1938	Single Payer
Germany	1941	Insurance Mandate
Belgium	1945	Insurance Mandate
United Kingdom	1948	Single Payer
Kuwait	1950	Single Payer
Sweden	1955	Single Payer
Bahrain	1957	Single Payer
Brunei	1958	Single Payer
Canada	1966	Single Payer
Netherlands	1966	Two Tier
Austria	1967	Insurance Mandate
United Arab Emirates	1971	Single Payer
Finland	1972	Single Payer
Slovenia	1972	Single Payer
Denmark	1973	Two Tier
Luxembourg	1973	Insurance Mandate
France	1974	Two Tier
Australia	1975	Two Tier
Ireland	1977	Two Tier
Italy	1978	Single Payer
Portugal	1979	Single Payer
Cyprus	1980	Single Payer
Greece	1983	Insurance Mandate

Country	Start Date of Universal Health Care	System Type
Spain	1986	Single Payer
South Korea	1988	Insurance Mandate
Iceland	1990	Single Payer
Hong Kong	1993	Two Tier
Singapore	1993	Two Tier
Switzerland	1994	Insurance Mandate
Israel	1995	Two Tier
United States	???	?

Data from this table was collected from *True Cost*, a blog on American policy, economics, and social issues: http://truecostblog.com/2009/08/09/countries-with-universal-healthcare-by-date/.

In 2007, the Commonwealth Fund ranked the health-care systems of seven developed nations based on overall performance. The nations evaluated included Australia, Germany, New Zealand, the Netherlands, Canada, and the United Kingdom. The health-care systems of these nations were evaluated for quality of care, access, efficiency, equity, quality of life, and health-care expenditures. The United States ranked last in the overall ranking and in almost every category. The average expenditure per patient in the United States was $7,290—almost double the expenditure of every other country included in the rankings, despite ranking seventh overall. In fact, the nation that ranked first, the Netherlands, spent a mere $3,837 per patient (Commonwealth Fund, 2010). We don't make the top grade in any of the measurable categories. What does the Netherlands have that we don't?

Ray Suarez and a *PBS NewsHour* reporting team sought to answer that question when they traveled to the Netherlands in 2009 to explore the country's innovative universal health-care system, which has gained attention as a potential model for US health-care reform. Below is a summary of what they learned and shared in their report (*PBS NewsHour*, 2009).

All residents of the Netherlands are required to purchase health insurance, which is provided by private health insurers that compete for business. The insurers can be either for-profit or nonprofit, but they are tightly regulated by the federal government and are required to accept every resident in their coverage area, regardless of preexisting conditions. The current system was created through a 2006 health policy reform. Prior to this, the country had a social health insurance system and a separate private health insurance alternative, neither of which exist any longer.

The government provides larger subsidies to insurers for participants who are sicker, elderly, or have preexisting conditions. Tax credits are given to low-income patients to help them purchase insurance. People under age eighteen are insured at no cost.

Patients can choose among the available insurers, but they often get their insurance through group plans administered by their employer. The Netherlands has a separate universal national social insurance program for long-term care, known as the AWBZ or Exceptional Medical Expenses Act.

Coverage

Legally required standard benefits for insurance in the Netherlands include general practitioners, hospitals, maternity care, lab tests, and medicines. Insurers offer a choice of policies at a range of costs. In some of the plans, the insurer negotiates and contracts with the health provider while more costly plans allow patients to choose their health provider and be reimbursed by the insurer. Most people also purchase additional private health insurance for services not covered, often from the insurer providing the basic coverage.

Financing

Government expenditure on health in the Netherlands made up 80 percent of health spending there in 2006, according to the World Health Organization. The required standard insurance is financed by a mixture of income-related contributions and flat premiums. The individual contribution is set at 6.5 percent of income, which is contributed by employers if the patient is enrolled through his or her job or by the individual if he or she is self-employed or unemployed. The insured also pay a flat-rate premium to their insurers for a policy. Everyone with the same policy pays the same premium, and lower-income residents receive a health-care allowance from the government to help make payments.

"What makes it most interesting from a US perspective is that it uses private insurers," says Michael Borowitz, a senior health policy analyst at the Organization for Economic Co-operation and Development in Paris. "[Instead of Medicaid and Medicare] the public insurance part is actually covered through private insurance, through the government regulating private insurers" (*PBS NewsHour*, 2009).

According to Niek Klazinga, professor of social medicine, Academic Medical Centre, University of Amsterdam, efficiency in the Dutch health-care system is promoted by providing regulated competition between insurers and transparency in outcomes via the use of performance indicators—measures of productivity that can be benchmarked against industry norms. This is complemented by a shift from a budget-based provider payment to a performance-based payment system (Klazinga, 2008).

There are other things that differentiate Dutch medicine from American medicine—for one, society's expectations and attitudes toward illness. The Dutch are much more stoic than we are. Most women have natural childbirth, without the use of epidural anesthesia or strong narcotic medication. Similarly, most family physicians will not prescribe unnecessary drugs for life's common aches and pains. Death and disease in the elderly are also treated much differently. A study conducted by the Centers for Medicare & Medicaid Services reported that in the United States, roughly 25 percent of one's lifelong health-care expenditure occurs in the last year of life (Calfo, 2008; Hogan, 2002; Lubitz, 1993). This is compared to 10 percent for the Dutch (Polder, 2006). The Dutch have a much more accepting attitude toward death. Euthanasia is legal in the Netherlands and a welcome method to end pain and suffering in terminally ill patients.

Medical malpractice is radically different in the United States compared to the Netherlands. An article published in the *European Journal of Emergency Medicine* (Elshove-Bolk J, 2004) provides a description of emergency department–related malpractice claims in the Netherlands. Between 1993 and 2001, a total of 326 claims involving the ED were filed at MediRisk (one of two big malpractice insurance carriers). That number is truly comical compared to the United States. According to *Plunkett's Insurance Industry Almanac*, in the state of Texas, 52 percent of physicians faced a malpractice lawsuit in the year 2000 (Plunkett, 2006). And in the Rio Grande Valley of Texas, the rate of malpractice suits was growing by 60 percent a year, with 350 suits for every 100 doctors!

Access to Care and Health Outcomes across the Globe

Let's continue to examine how the United States compares to other countries across the globe when it comes to access to care and health outcomes.

In 2010, the United States outspent all of the other thirty-four countries currently tracked by the Organization for Economic Co-operation and Development (OECD) by a sizable margin, with an average health spending per capita of $8,233. This was two-and-a-half times more than the average expenditure per capita of $3,268 of all thirty-five nations tracked by the OECD. As a share of GDP, the United States spent 17.6 percent on health. This was 5 percentage points more than in the next three countries, the Netherlands, France, and Germany, which spent 12 percent and 11.6 percent (France and Germany) of their GDP on health (OECD, 2012).

Recent health data, also from the OECD, compared the United States to ten countries on a variety of points related to access to care and outcomes. Countries included Germany, Italy, Australia, France, Canada, the Netherlands, the United Kingdom, New Zealand, Switzerland, and Sweden. From the study, one can conclude that the United States does not set a good standard for health and health care when compared to its peers, despite having high health-care expenditures.

The United States ranks at the bottom on the number of annual physician visits per citizen, 3.8, with the median being 6.3 and the highest at 13.2 in Japan. This may reflect an emphasis on health maintenance in other countries and could contribute to the decreased cost of health care as disease is prevented rather than cured (Commonwealth Fund, 2010).

Next the OECD examined the potential years of life lost due to diabetes per 100,000 people. You guessed it—the United States ranks first out of the eleven countries with the greatest number of years lost due to diabetes (Commonwealth Fund, 2009). The difference between the United States (ninety-nine years) and New Zealand (sixty-four years), which ranks second, is staggering! Diabetes is rampant in the United States and is obviously taking a huge toll on life expectancy. Despite spending more on health care than any of the other countries on the chart, we fall way behind when it comes to controlling diabetes.

The United States also leads the pack in obesity (BMI > 30) and its numerous associated diseases. I attribute this to economic prosperity, social welfare, lifestyle influences, and cultural beliefs and practices.

The report also found that we rank last in increasing life expectancy (Commonwealth Fund, 2008), despite spending more on health care, having some of the best universities in the world, and generating some of the most prolific research.

In 2010, the Commonwealth Fund presented the rate of cost-related problems with access to health care among eight countries, including the United States. Cost-related problems with access to care may prevent a patient from filling a prescription, visiting a doctor with a medical problem, or getting a recommended test, treatment, or follow-up. The report found that the United States consistently ranked last, with the highest percentage of chronically ill adults reporting that they did not receive care within the last year due to cost (Commonwealth Fund, 2010).

I have shown you that in most other developed countries that were ranked, health-care delivery is better overall and costs less. The next big question is, "Why is this so?" I will answer that in the next chapter, "Drivers of Health-Care Costs."

Chapter 3:
Drivers of Health-Care Costs

Good Care Costs Money

As I said earlier, good health-care costs money. Good care that is delivered in an unaccountable way costs more money. Good care that is delivered in an environment of fear of retribution costs even more money. Computerized axial tomography (CAT) scans, magnetic resonance imaging (MRI), and positron emission tomography (PET) scans didn't just develop themselves one day. It took a lot of research and development capital to develop these sophisticated testing modalities. Similarly, it costs a lot to build and maintain them, so naturally they cost a lot of money, and that cost is passed on to the consumer.

Likewise, the pharmaceutical industry allocates tremendous resources to research and development of new drugs. Sophisticated medical and surgical procedures may be very complex and cost lots and lots of money (e.g., bone marrow transplants, open heart surgery, and transplant surgery). For example, the total cost per patient for a heart transplant in the United States is an estimated $787,000. The cost for a liver transplant is $523,400, and a kidney transplant is $259,000 (United Network for Organ Sharing, 2012). Compare that to the advertised price for a kidney transplant package in India for around $7,500 USD. This is significantly cheaper than it would cost in the United States (Travel India Company, 2006). (I will elaborate further on the medical sales and pharmaceutical industries in chapter 5.)

Lack of Integration

Since the 1930s, the US government has been looking at ways to reduce the cost of health care. In 1932, the Committee on Costs of Medical Care called for a Mayo Model, calling for an integrated multispecialty group practice modeled after the Mayo Clinic (Committee on the Costs of Medical Care, 1932). They identified the lack of efficiency in the fee-for-service model. Again, in 2001, the Institute of Medicine's report, *Crossing the Quality Chasm*, called for:

1. Reform of the health-care delivery process
2. Effective use of information technology
3. Development of effective health-care teams
4. Coordination of care across patient conditions, services, and settings over time
5. Setting performance standards
6. Performance and outcome measurements for improvement and accountability (Institute of Medicine, 2001)

According to the *Dartmouth Atlas of Health Care* and the Centers for Medicare & Medicaid Services, there is significant variation in health-care costs across the United States. The most interesting finding is that there was no correlation in quality outcomes with the amount of money spent; actually, there is evidence to suggest that quality outcomes are better in lower-spending regions. Furthermore, integrated group practice organizations—such as the Mayo Clinic—delivered better quality care at a lower price (*Dartmouth Atlas of Health Care*, 2012), comparing apples to apples and measuring quality of care by common measures of health-care performance, such as adherence to best standards of care, practicing evidence-based medicine, etc.

This makes intuitive sense. The fee-for-service model is a free-for-all. In this model, there is no medical home for the patient. Care is delivered in a fragmented way according to the wants of any physician involved in the care process. Specialist consultations are provided when there is not a definite need for them. Tests and radiological imaging studies are ordered endlessly without any accountability. And finally, physicians' income is dependent on the extent of services provided; the more you do, the more you get.

Now compare this to an integrated group practice model where patients have a medical home. All of the service providers are on the same team, marching to the beat of the same drummer, sharing an organizational culture and philosophy. There is a unified medical record, with everyone being able to access the same record and review workups that have been done, eliminating the need for repetitive testing. Quality performance and outcome measures are more likely to be in place in a large multispecialty group practice, ensuring adherence to best practice and evidence-based medicine guidelines. And finally, physicians are not rewarded for the number of tests they order or procedures they perform. Rather, they are salaried with performance incentives based on productivity, adherence to practice guidelines, and economic credentialing (which is the cost of delivering care compared to peers with similar outcomes).

Such large, integrated organizations have economies of scale, making it easier to implement costly technologies like electronic medical records, which could be too costly for individual practitioners to purchase. There is more uniformity because all team members are going to be using the same EMR, whereas in independent practices, each practitioner will choose what he or she wants, making integration a logistical nightmare.

Mental Masturbation

Got your attention there, didn't I? I'm not being funny or crude. This is a real problem in the practice of medicine. I told you that some of my colleagues will be offended by this book, and this is partially why. I am about to rain down a barrage of criticism on my intellectual colleagues.

I have the utmost respect for all physicians. It is a rare breed of individual who can dedicate his or her life to the practice of medicine. Having said that, I will also tell you that there is an inbred culture of endless and useless testing of patients to rule out the presence of the rarest, most obscure illness. As a surgeon, at the end of the day, when I reflect upon my work, regardless of how mundane an operation I performed or how fancy, I have definitive, concrete evidence as to the results of my work and its influence upon my patient's life. Yes, I spend time contemplating rare illnesses, working patients up before surgery, and caring for them after surgery, but the bulk of my impact occurs in the operating room.

We teach our medical students to think of horses when they hear hoofbeats, not zebras. Common things are common. Uncommon presentations of common things are more common than common presentations of uncommon things! This age-old dictum seems to have been lost on our nonsurgical colleagues. The highlight of their day is discussing the rarest of diseases among the differential diagnoses and proving they don't exist.

When an infant goes to the emergency department with a febrile seizure, it is often automatically assumed that the patient is suffering from bacterial meningitis until proven otherwise. The most common cause of seizures in infants is a high fever, plain and simple. The most common causes of high fevers are viral infections or simple bacterial infections, not bacterial meningitis. Nonetheless, said poor child is going to get a lumbar puncture to test the cerebrospinal fluid for bacterial meningitis. This is an uncomfortable and costly procedure with a positive study yield rate of zero in certain studies (Kimia A, 2010). Extrapolate this kind of thinking across the majority of patient encounters, and you can see how quickly this can turn into a witch hunt. I wish there were a reliable source that tracked the number of unnecessary studies I could quote from, but there isn't. This observation comes from personal observation and opinion that is shared by surgical colleagues across the spectrum.

This behavior is reinforced and rewarded in our training programs to sharpen our students' minds and make sure they consider all possibilities. This kind of thinking has generated its own culture among younger physicians. Young doctors in training have a free range to order any test they deem necessary to rule out whichever disease they are considering without consequence or accountability. When I was in training in the '80s and '90s, CAT scans were ordered selectively, usually after serious considerations and consultations with senior members of the care team to address specific issues. Now they have become a routine screening tool that is ordered on nearly each and every person presenting to the hospital with abdominal pain. Surgeons used to order these studies if they felt they needed to, but now they are done before a surgeon ever sees the patient. Despite the increased utilization of CAT scans, there is no evidence that they have improved patient care when used in this fashion. According to one study,[7] CAT scan utilization in the emergency department has increased by 330 percent over the last

---

[7] Keith Kocher, MD, MPH, William J. Meurer, MD, et al., "National Trends in Use of Computed Tomography in the Emergency Department." *Annals of Emergency Medicine*, 58 (2011): 452–62.e3.

decade. This is not to mention the further workups and investigations for evaluating other incidentally discovered findings that are usually meaningless. Some authors have referred to this state as "VOMIT"—victim of modern imaging technology.

The diagnostic skills physicians used to have that were honed by years of careful, thorough clinical patient evaluation in the previous generation have been eroded away by the advent of modern testing. Clinicians frequently treat abnormal test results rather than treating their patient. Modern medicine readily embraces newer, more sophisticated technology in the belief that it *must* improve patient care.

A case in point is mammography X-rays of the breast to detect early cancers. Current recommendations are for screening mammography to begin at age forty unless there is a higher risk of breast cancer, in which case screening can start earlier (American Cancer Society, 2012). This has been the standard of care for several decades. Needless to say, mammograms identify early cancers, but they also identify lots of other noncancerous pathology. It doesn't stop there. Abnormal mammograms also lead to more testing (ultrasounds and MRIs, for example) and frequently X-ray or ultrasound-guided biopsies or open surgical biopsies. The majority of these biopsies reveal benign, noncancerous disease, yet millions of women have been subjected to "the standard of care."

There are several studies (at least eight out of Canada, Sweden, Denmark, and the United States, to name a few) that have proven that routine screening mammography does not change the outcome of breast cancer patients. Yes, you read right. Mammography does not influence breast cancer mortality. According to the National Breast Cancer Coalition, screening mammography may improve survival by a mere 0.05 percent (National Breast Cancer Coalition, 2011)! That means that five out of every ten thousand patients may have an advantage from obtaining a mammogram with regard to surviving breast cancer. You don't see this information being disseminated to the public or even being taught to our medical students and residents. How many millions of dollars have we spent? How many patients have we subjected to unnecessary anxiety, and how many needless biopsies have been performed—all in the name of the standard of care? When are we going to learn? We preach evidence-based medicine from the rooftops of our watchdog institutions but do not practice what we preach.

I'm not suggesting that we abolish the practice of mammography but simply to redefine the indications. Screening mammography would be used only for high-risk patients and diagnostic mammography for clinically suspicious conditions. Now continue along this line of reasoning and extrapolate these recommendations across the spectrum of the practice of medicine. Let's be realistic. There are billions of dollars to be saved in unnecessary testing. Of course, there is another factor influencing such practices, and that is the legal implications in our litigious society, but that's a loaded topic that I'll save for later.

Sociocultural Influences

The United States leads the world in higher education, followed by Sweden and then Canada.[8] The majority of the world's top higher education institutions reside in the United States. Our GDP is heads and shoulders above our closest competitor, China, followed by Japan and then India.[9]

Given these facts, one would think they would reflect favorably on the profile of the typical health-care consumer, right? *Not!* You can Google it if you want, but I can tell you that everywhere I have practiced (in several different areas of Texas, New York, and Washington), the lion's share of health-care costs were spent on people of lower socioeconomic status, of lower educational achievements, and of certain cultural backgrounds. Please be advised: there is no prejudice or stereotyping here, just years of personal observation; just facts.

Economically and educationally underdeveloped segments of our society by definition have more health issues and rely on emergency room services more than citizens who are better off. They are also less likely to be insured or to rely on Medicaid or Medicare coverage. Mexican Americans and African Americans are represented more frequently in this patient subgroup than in the affluent privately insured population (30.4 percent of Hispanics, 17 percent of blacks, and 9.9 percent of whites do not have health insurance).[10]

Let me bring Abraham Maslow's Hierarchy of Needs into the discussion. Maslow was an American psychologist who stratified

---

[8] U21 Rankings of National Higher Education, Accessed June 24, 2012, http://www.universitas21.com/link/U21Rankings.

[9] Index Mundi, "GDP, Purchasing Power Parity," Accessed June 24, 2012, www.indexmundi.com/g/r.aspx?t=50&v=65.

[10] Centers for Disease Control and Prevention, "People without Health Insurance Coverage, by Race and Ethnicity," Accessed June 24, 2012, www.cdc.gov/Features/dsHealthInsurance.

people's needs based on the progressive impact of those needs on their lives (Maslow, 1943). The needs are often represented in a pyramid, with five levels of needs: physiological, safety, love/belonging, esteem, and self-actualization. At the base of the pyramid are the most basic needs of human beings (physiological needs and safety), and at the top are the more esoteric, higher order needs of esteem and self-actualization.

Okay, how do I say this in a politically correct way? Oh, wait a moment! I promised you that I was not going to be PC. Here it is: most of my patients who consume the majority of our health-care dollars are living to fulfill needs on the lower half of this pyramid. I'm sorry, but it's just a fact. I have reached this conclusion based on years of clinical practice in various venues across the United States. As a matter of fact, the lower people are on the pyramid, the higher their medical needs. Similarly, the lower they are, the more likely their lifestyle choices are contributing to their health-care needs.

To simplify it further, the bottom of the pyramid is a homeless guy. The top is someone who wants to achieve his or her life's goal of working for the Peace Corps with a PhD in sociology. The patient who wants a breast augmentation, on average, is going to be a healthy, productive member of society who is going to pay cash for the procedure, costing the average citizen nothing at all. She is more likely to be situated closer to the top of the pyramid than the next example I'm about to give you—a twenty-five-year-old, unemployed gang member who got shot by the cops in a robbery attempt. His care is financed by you and me. He offers nothing in the way of payment, has no secure job, and has no insurance, so you and I carry the bill!

If I get called to the ER at 2:00 a.m. for a trauma patient, I can pretty much guarantee it's not going to be a college professor but more likely an unemployed, drunk, tattooed individual who does not have a college education and is not insured. I'm sorry, but these are just the facts. Similarly, most of the consults I get in the emergency room of a large, academically associated hospital for surgical management of disease are on patients of low socioeconomic and educational status, a large majority of who are obese or morbidly obese, with multiple medical problems. That's not to say that employed people don't have emergency health issues. I am just presenting the facts I have garnered from years of experience across the country that clearly demonstrate that the lion's share of emergency department health care is delivered to people of lower socioeconomic status.

This patient population is less likely to make regular doctor visits for health maintenance, and they are more likely to practice self-destructive lifestyle choices. Morbid obesity, diabetes, high blood pressure, high cholesterol, heart disease, and cancer, to name a few, are more prevalent illnesses in this patient group. So I guess we can write it all off and attribute these chronic diseases to their genes. Sure, part of it is genetic no doubt, but what about the other part?

There is a huge movement in this country to involve patients in their own medical care. Patients are encouraged to ask questions about their illnesses, partake in decision making, and be part of the team. Informed consent has to be obtained prior to any intervention, meaning that patients must be made to understand their disease process, the various treatment options, the risks and potential complications of the proposed treatment, and the risk of not pursuing treatment. What about patients' involvement in disease prevention? Does the fact that their culture tolerates, and may even encourage, obesity factor in to the equation? How about lack of exercise and poor food choices? Alcohol and tobacco use? What about lack of early medical intervention for illnesses rather than letting them fester for years before they are addressed? Where does a patient's involvement in these issues begin and end?

Unfortunately, this is a lost cause. Despite a ton of research and outreach programs by well-intended activists, the problem is only getting worse, not better. Obesity and childhood obesity are on the rise, not the decline. I have yet to see any meaningful impact on the culturally predetermined eating and lifestyle habits by any intervention. I'm sorry, but reaching out to a Hispanic "Colonia" in the Rio Grande Valley of South Texas or an African American "ghetto" community in New York with educational brochures, social worker visits, and various other outreach programs is simply not effective.[11]

Pizzas, sloppy joes, corn dogs, burritos, nondiet soft drinks, cookies, candy, cheeseburgers, mac and cheese, chicken nuggets, and fried chicken still populate common food choices in our public schools. Where is the government's responsibility in providing healthy food choices to our kids?

To compound matters, this segment of the population is growing at a much faster rate than the higher socioeconomic status segment.

---

11 Centers for Disease Control and Prevention, "Compared with whites, Blacks had 51% higher and Hispanics had 21% higher obesity rates," Accessed June 24, 2012, www.cdc.gov/Features/dsObesityAdults.

Minorities in general account for the most rapid expansion in population, and Hispanics account for more than half of the population growth between 2000 and 2010 (US Census Bureau, 2011). This is only going to compound things further over time as more and more of our population joins the ranks of the unemployed who are socially and culturally underdeveloped. Mind you, I am not saying that Latinos are all unemployed, but the fact is they represent a higher percentage of the unemployed population; similarly, Latinos are least likely to pursue higher education (US Census Bureau, 2012). Blacks and Hispanics account for the majority of the population categorized as being in poverty (US Census Bureau, 2012, white 13 percent, black 36 percent, Hispanic 35 percent).[12]

But there is more to the problem than just the cost of health care for this segment of society. The state perpetuates the status quo by providing the welfare umbrella. The unemployed poverty status is rewarded with emergency Medicaid, food stamps, TANF (temporary aid for needy families), EITC (earned income tax credit), WIC (nutrition program for women, infants, and children), CHIP (children's health insurance program), and other entitlement programs that cost the country 13.62 percent of its federal spending in 2003.

Mind you, I am not suggesting that we leave the poor to fend for themselves; quite the contrary. I do believe in a social welfare umbrella. There is no reason why one of the most developed countries in the world should have citizens who cannot afford health care. Much to the chagrin of many of my colleagues, I do believe in a government-mandated and -funded safety net to take care of our uninsured or high-risk patients who do not have mandated insurance coverage.

But at the same time, I have seen too many welfare recipients linger on for the tremendous benefits provided by these entitlement programs. There should be a catch, but there isn't. Entitlement programs should come with a caveat. The government is here to help, but you need to help yourself too. Perpetuation of this state should not be encouraged or allowed. No welfare recipient should be allowed to receive benefits as long as he or she can physically participate in the work force. I don't care what the job is: street sweeper, shoe shiner, federal cafeteria employee, license plate stamper, librarian, rocket scientist, or whatever. As long as there is unemployment and there are jobs to be filled, people should

---

12   Poverty Rate by Race/Ethnicity, Accessed June 24, 2012, www.statehealthfacts.org/comparebar.jsp?ind=14&cat=1.

work for what they get. If there is an unfilled job ad, it must be given to the recipient for him or her to be allowed to receive government subsidies.

Subsidized education programs should be part of the package. If you do not have a marketable skill, it is the duty of the government to provide you with one based upon your particular aptitudes. Citizens should be rehabilitated to allow them to become productive members of society. Whether it is a vocational degree, a GED, or a college degree, one needs to have something to allow participation in the work force. A perpetual state of entitlement should not be an option, as it is now!

Currently we reward poverty, unemployment, and multiple children with no means to support them with a litany of benefits without any conditions. According to Arloc Sherman from the Center on Budget and Policy Priorities (8/2005), public assistance programs reduce the number of poor Americans by twenty seven million people, including fourteen million elderly and five million children. These programs also decrease the severity of poverty by increasing the average disposable income from 29 percent to 57 percent of the poverty line and offer health insurance to tens of millions of Americans. These public programs consist of two main categories: income support regardless of level of income and means-tested benefits, which provide assistance to people of low or modest income.

- Income support: Social Insurance—social security, unemployment insurance, and workers' compensation.
- Means-tested benefits: TANF (temporary assistance for needy families), SSI (supplemental security income), food stamps, school lunch, rental assistance, and energy assistance.
- Refundable Tax Credits: EITC (earned income tax credit), child tax credit.
- Health Insurance: Medicaid for low income patients, Medicare for disabled and senior patients and SCHIP (state children's health insurance plan).

Timothy Smeeding, a leading figure on public benefit programs in developed countries, conducted research revealing that government assistance programs lift one of every nine low-income children to half the national median income in the United States compared to one of every three in Canada and one of two in Britain, Germany, the Netherlands, Belgium, and other developed countries, despite the United States having the largest GDP of all.[13]

So many of my Medicaid patients are unemployed yet living a fairly relaxed lifestyle, as evidenced by their obesity, their multiple children, and the gold chains and hickeys on their necks! Some elderly patients in my practice are provided with a home provider—a caretaker to assist with activities of daily life when they have unemployed children who can provide this care!

We also punish productivity. If you are unemployed, your chances of getting emergency Medicaid are much better than if you have a low-paying job. I have seen many of my working patients who are barely scraping by holding down a low-paying job get turned down for any kind of subsidized insurance program because they make "too much money" when they are living a meager existence, unable to afford private health insurance. They definitely cannot afford the cost of their health care. The government's solution is for them to quit their job so they can be eligible. Seems very logical, doesn't it? This must be something that our all-knowing government would come up with. I have also had patients approved for emergency Medicaid for supposed life-threatening illnesses, yet I have had unfunded patients turned down for treatment of breast cancer. Go figure—our government at work again. I wonder if the clerk realizes that breast cancer is a life-threatening illness!

Another sociocultural attitude I have observed over the years is the willingness (or lack thereof) of family members to participate in providing home patient care. The weed-like growth of the home health industry feeds on the attitude that families have toward caring for their loved ones. So many patients end up getting home health services they don't need because it is available and paid for by Medicare or Medicaid, and they do not have to spend a cent out of pocket. Home health services artificially increase their value by padding their services to include such meaningless and lofty goals as educating a patient about the symptoms and signs of diabetes when the patient has been diabetic for thirty years and the nurse's job is to provide dressing changes for a surgical wound.

---

13 Timothy M. Smeeding, "Children in America: A Comparative View of Our Nation's Future," Population Resource Center Congressional Seminar, Washington, DC, December 9, 2004.

I turn down so many requests for home health services that I never requested. They are usually requested by family members and approved by primary care physicians trying to keep families happy. When they come across my desk and I see the absurdity of their requests and plans, I turn them down. Some people really do need home health services, but the majority of these services are unnecessary. It's a racket costing taxpayers millions of dollars. I estimate that 50 to 60 percent of services can be eliminated by having patients and family members participate in the care process. I'm not talking about complex medical interventions at all, just simple, commonsense things most people can do, such as simple wound care.

The Billing Bureaucracy

Medical billing used to be very simple. One presented to the doctor with a particular complaint and got evaluated. A treatment plan was implemented, and the patient was responsible for the bill. Insurance companies usually took care of the bill with doctors' invoices. Now it takes a plethora of workers filling endless insurance claims that are denied and resubmitted with further documentation to appease the purse-string holders as to the validity of the claim.

The complexities of the medical coding system are so egregious that physicians are constantly looking over their shoulders to make sure they are not violating any governmental rules because the consequences could have serious financial ramifications, with hefty fines being levied against the offending doctors regardless of whether he over- or under-coded for the encounter. The billing code assigned to a particular patient encounter depends on whether the patient is a new or established patient and whether he or she is being referred by another physician for a consultation. The complexity of the encounter is judged by the severity of the problem or problems, the time it took to evaluate the patient, the level of detail that is involved in obtaining the patient's history, the number of body systems evaluated, and so on. There is a different set of codes for office encounters and hospital encounters, and the rules of conduct are so complicated that it is impossible to know for certain if the chosen code is the right one. Meanwhile, if you ask five different Medicare coding specialists, they will give you five different answers as to how you should process this information and deal with it.

Then there is the problem of preauthorization. Peter is a sixty-six-year-old man I operated on several weeks ago. He suffered from advanced diabetes, high blood pressure, dialysis-dependent renal failure, and poor circulation. I was consulted while he was in the hospital on the medical service to evaluate him for a chronic, ulcerated, infected left-foot wound. It was determined that he needed to undergo a below-the-knee amputation, which he underwent without incident. He was eventually discharged to a rehabilitative facility.

He came to my clinic for his follow-up appointment after surgery. Unfortunately, his wound was infected and was displaying signs of insufficient blood supply. I determined that Peter needed to be admitted to the hospital for intravenous antibiotics and more surgery. I was also concerned about his diabetes, which could be seriously impacted by the wound infection that had set in.

Just one problem—Peter is a veteran's administration (VA) patient. The VA does not have an inpatient hospital in our area, so they contract with one of the local community hospitals to take care of VA patients. I wrote up his admission orders and had the office call the hospital to arrange for an admission, only to be told by the hospital staff that the VA had to preauthorize the admission. We dutifully called the local VA preauthorization office, only to be told that we had to call the patient's outpatient VA clinic and talk to his provider to obtain preauthorization. We dutifully called that number ... and it rang and rang and rang, with no one answering the phone. We then called the preauthorization number again and were told that their hands were tied and they couldn't help us. I explained that this patient was in serious trouble and needed to be admitted to the hospital, but it was out of their hands. We were told to keep trying the outpatient clinic and talk to his provider, which we did several times, without success. There was not even a voicemail option.

I can't say I'm surprised because this has been a common occurrence with the VA. The VA is bogged down with such a quagmire of red tape that patients don't always get the streamlined care they deserve. Their care is frequently interrupted by lengthy preauthorization procedures.

Sam is a VA patient I saw in consultation for a narrowed blood vessel in his neck, the carotid artery, which supplies his brain with blood. The narrowing had diminished the blood supply enough to cause him to have a stroke. While I took his history, I found he had been suffering from warning signs of transient ischemic attacks—mini, reversible strokes—for months. His primary doctor had evaluated him with a Doppler ultrasound, a noninvasive study that uses sound waves to evaluate the artery. He was found to have critical narrowing of the blood vessel that required urgent surgery to avoid a stroke. That was six months prior! Sam didn't get the authorization in time to see a vascular surgeon before he developed a stroke. Thank you, VA!

Legal Influences

Okay, I've saved the best for last. There is no question that our current legal system is driving up the cost of health care. If a society has to put up with such nonsense as having to print warnings about the lead content of fish hooks on the box in case of accidental swallowing (which I've personally seen), then something is terribly wrong. Common sense and personal responsibility are no longer allowed! Lawyers have found a way to erode the very basic foundations of common sense and personal responsibility by attacking anything and everything they can make a dime off.

A lawsuit is filed every two seconds in the United States (Center for America/PBS Wacky Warning Labels). The spinoff? All the stupid crap that you see every day: the sign stating that the stone-lined walkway in the park is uneven, so watch your step; the accept button on your car's GPS stating that you won't program it while driving; the list of risks and possible complications of a drug on a TV ad lasting longer than the information about the drug itself; the sign on the jungle gym warning you about the risks of falling; the warning about not using the car's speakerphone that you bought while driving; not using the toilet brush for personal hygiene—I think you get the picture. If you want more entertainment, I refer you to *Remove Child before Folding: the 101 Stupidest, Silliest, and Wackiest Warning Labels Ever*, by Bob Dorigo, or just Google "wackiest warning labels," and I guarantee you a good, heartfelt laugh. That is the underlying legal mind-set in this country. If you have to warn a guy about the lead content of his fish hooks, just think about what kind of warnings you have to put on a medical or surgical consent form.

The first problem we have is the tremendous number of lawyers practicing in the United States today. There are many reasons for this. First, the United States continues to lead other nations as the world's leading jailer. In fact, a report released by the International Centre for Prison Studies indicates that almost half of the world's incarcerated are being held in correctional facilities in the United States, despite the fact that the United States has less than 5 percent of the world's total population (Walmsley, 2009). The Bureau of Justice Statistics reports that state and federal correctional facilities were housing 1,605,127 prisoners at the end of 2010 (Guerino, 2011).

The economic impact of the rate of growth of our prison population, especially the rate of growth of the elderly baby boomer generation detainees, has skyrocketed out of control. Department of Justice statistics show that the number of inmates in federal and state prisons age fifty-five and older shot up 33 percent from 2000 to 2005, the most recent year for which the data was available. That's faster than the 9 percent growth overall. Rising prison health-care costs—particularly for elderly inmates—helped fuel a 10 percent jump in state prison spending from fiscal year 2005 to 2006, according to the National Conference of State Legislatures. That growth in spending is projected to continue. You see, inmate health care is a constitutional right, unlike for hardworking, productive citizens!

Is it surprising that the highest percentage of our prisoners, by race, is also part of the fastest-growing segment of our population by race? Latinos and African Americans represent the highest percentage of our system's inmates and similarly represent the fastest-growing segment of our population. This means that we as a society will continue to spend more and more money on inmates as the minority section of our population outgrows the rest. This will further contribute to the cost of health-care delivery.

According to the report, *US Tort Costs and Cross Border Perspectives* published by Towers Watson, a global professional services firm that helps organizations improve performance through effective people and risk and financial management, the United States leads the world in estimated tort costs as percentage of GDP (Towers Watson [Perrin], 2006). The most recent data from Towers Watson indicates that nearly 2 percent of GDP in the United States comes from tort-associated costs (Towers Watson, 2010). Given the above statistic, it should come as no surprise that the United States has the highest number of lawyers per capita in the world, 1/265 (ABA). The seven highest "lawyerly" countries in descending order are the United States, Brazil, New Zealand, Spain, Italy, UK, Germany, and France (ABA, Brazilian ABA equivalent OAB, Council of European Lawyers). Of these seven countries, the United States has 50 percent of all lawyers. We are by far the most litigious country in the world. This mind-set permeates our lives and touches every facet of our society, the medical sector not excluded.

Medical Malpractice

As I mentioned earlier, according to *Plunkett's Insurance Industry Almanac*, in the state of Texas in the year 2000, 52 percent of physicians faced a malpractice lawsuit. In the Rio Grande Valley of Texas, the rate of malpractice suits was growing by 60 percent a year, with 350 suits for every 100 doctors! Keep in mind that these figures reflect the situation *after* tort reform was enacted in Texas limiting noneconomic damages to a $250,000 cap (Plunkett, 2006).

Lawyers defend *contingency fees*—legal payment based on a percent of winnings (no win, no pay)—as a measure to make legal representation affordable to citizens who couldn't otherwise afford the cost of a lawsuit. That is a very interesting position since the practice of contingency fees is not allowed in family or criminal law. What about the poor guy going through a divorce or the guy wronged by a bad business deal? Doesn't he deserve representation? Is it any coincidence that the highest rewards are given in personal injury/malpractice suits? Contingency fees are seen as unethical in many countries and are not allowed except in personal injury/malpractice and workman's compensation cases in the United States.

In all other compensation models, the amount of compensation is calculated based on the amount of time and effort involved and the complexity of the task at hand. I get paid a fixed amount (often reduced from my asking fee) for performing an operation. I also get to charge more if I'm doing a more complex operation. Similarly your car mechanic will charge you a fixed price for an oil change or a transmission job. Your business attorney will charge you an hourly rate for drawing up articles of incorporation or a legal contract. So why then does a malpractice attorney get to charge a fee based on the amount of winnings? The answer is very obvious. It is an enticement for attorneys to take on these cases and take home huge fees as a percentage of collections.

Lawyers will accept contingency payments on cases they expect to win, with no obligation to do the same for low-merit cases. So much for caring about the poor. They also justify exorbitant awards based on such factors as pain and suffering, lost wages, and lost earning potential on behalf of the plaintiff and lost companionship and financial support on behalf of the plaintiff's family.

Okay, I get it. Let's extrapolate that argument a bit. If I get called in at 3:00 a.m. to take care of a wealthy thirty-five-year-old businessman who was stabbed in a mugging and I operate on him and save his life,

Health-Care Reform: A Surgeon's Perspective

then I could argue that I should get paid more than if I were to save the life of a sixty-year-old unemployed, uninsured, homeless alcoholic. Let's see, the argument applies just as well. If I had not gotten my butt out of bed (and incurred pain and suffering), then the businessman would be dead. By saving his life, I have allowed him to continue to earn his usual earnings, have avoided pain and suffering on the part of his family, and have avoided the lack of financial support enjoyed by his family, and therefore I should be rewarded accordingly with a formula based on earning potential over the years of life that I have saved him and the absence of pain and suffering and financial hardship his family would have incurred if I hadn't done my job.

But that's not the way it works. I charge a service fee for the amount of time, effort, and expertise I provide based on a fixed payment schedule that is determined by the government. But wait, there's more. I don't get to charge my consultation fee for coming in and evaluating the patient if I take him to surgery the same day. Wait, there's more. I also get to take care of this patient for free for the next three months in an arrangement the government calls a global fee arrangement.

The sixty-year-old guy? Nah, he was a useless member of society! Is that what lawyers are trying to tell us here? Based on legal logic, I shouldn't get paid as much for saving his behind, and I should have the option of not accepting him as my patient because my financial incentives are nonexistent. I also don't have the luxury of turning down a case because I think it's going to be complicated. I am legally obliged to accept this patient because I happen to be on call for unassigned patients that present to my hospital, regardless of their ability to pay their bill. I can't turn them down. Furthermore, I can get fined for refusing to treat or accept a patient who needs my services. Mind you, I am not a government employee. I don't work for the department of justice or health and human services, and I am a private practice physician. Yet the *law* obliges me to accept patients regardless of their ability to pay my bill. Yet I am still liable for anything that might go wrong with my patients' medical treatment.

You know what? I never went into medicine to make a lot of money. I love what I do. It is a privilege to be allowed to take care of a human being with the impact that I have on peoples' lives. Mind you, I like being paid for what I do, but at the same time, I am not about to turn down patients whose lives depend on what I can offer them because they can't pay my bill—especially not in an emergency.

There are all these built-in rules that mandate care for patients suffering from a serious medical problem. Why, might I ask you, are there not similar governmental regulations to see for the care of citizens in need of legal counseling? If the American Bar Association's stand is that contingency fees are there for poor citizens so that they can access the legal system, then why do they not provide for all citizens who need emergency legal care that might impact the rest of their lives, whether it is a divorce matter or a business matter? The answer is very obvious. There is no financial incentive for lawyers to take on the case unless there is a significant amount of money involved for them. So unless a lawyer is working for the government where he has to take on unassigned cases in the prosecution or defense venue, there is no legal obligation to provide free services. Yet I am held to a different standard. I have to take care of patients regardless of their ability to pay for their services.

Another argument for contingency fees is the increased motivation for the attorney to work harder at winning the case if he gets paid more. Okay, let's take that argument a little further. In that case, I should have an incentive payment plan to work harder to ensure a successful outcome for my patient. If you survive an operation, then I get to charge a higher rate than if you croak or have a complication! Ludicrous, isn't it? A doctor should do his job regardless of the financial remuneration, the best that he can to save his patient. That's the only moral and ethical thing to do, right? So I ask you, why is a lawyer any different?

The percentage of winnings the attorney takes is up for negotiation. It is customary to charge 30 to 40 percent. Different states have different statutes, some allowing a progressive sliding scale contingency for progressively higher awards, whereas some states do not cap the percentage of the award that can go to the attorney (American Bar Association/Department of Justice).

In England, conditional fees, as they are known there, are usually in addition to the solicitor's hourly rate and are capped off at no more than 100 percent of the solicitor's fee. Conditional fees are usually in the range of 25 percent of the fee. In contrast, the American Bar Association is in staunch opposition to both caps on noneconomic damages and caps on contingency fees. Interestingly, former President George W. Bush banned contingency fees from governmental legal dealings.

As of 2011, seventeen states in the United States have specific limits on contingency fees. Among them are populous states such as

California, Florida, New York, and Illinois. Twenty states have no limits on contingency fees, including Texas (National Conference of State Legislatures, 2011).

States that have caps on contingency fees have a higher percentage of dropped malpractice cases (American Enterprise Institute for Public Policy research). The American Medical Association has demonstrated that in states that cap noneconomic damages, malpractice insurance rates rose less than in states that did not have caps. Similarly, physician per capita rates increased in states that had caps.

It is no secret that the current malpractice crisis has influenced the availability of physician services in numerous counties across the states. Right here in my backyard in Texas, I have seen our communities become underserved in the area of neurosurgical care. Other counties have lost all their obstetricians, so women have to travel far away from home to receive obstetrical care.

According to the American Medical Association, defensive medicine practice adds between $84 to $151 billion dollars a year to the cost of health care. Approximately 60 percent of lawsuits against physicians are dropped, withdrawn, or dismissed, yet the cost of each one of these was about $22,000 to defend in 2008. Physicians are not found negligent in over 90 percent of cases that do go to trial, costing more than $110,000 dollars each to defend (Guardado, 2009). So let's do the math. Of one hundred suits filed, sixty are thrown out, leaving forty to go to trial. Of these, 90 percent (thirty-six) are found not guilty, leaving four cases out of one hundred that are rewarded damages!

Medical liability premiums have increased 1,029 percent in the United States from 1976 to 2007 except in California, where they have increased by less than a third of that due to tort reform setting caps on noneconomic damages (American Medical Association, 2010). Again I say, so much for the lawyers caring for the poor! They are in it for the money, plain and simple.

Let's move on beyond contingency fees. How about the manner in which malpractice cases are managed? A disgruntled patient or family member contacts a lawyer with a grievance. The lawyer evaluates the merit of the case and renders an opinion regarding its likelihood of success. The patient or representative is usually reassured that the damages are not coming out of the doctor's pocket. The insurance company is there to take care of that. The way is paved for a suit, and awards are anticipated. A contingency fee is arranged so the plaintiff is out nothing.

Then the process begins. Expert witnesses are drummed up to support the plaintiff's case. Some of these expert witnesses are hired guns. Supposedly experts in their field but frequently on the take, these are expert prostitutes who will sell their mothers for a dime. Through personal lawsuit experience and from serving as an expert witness for the defense in malpractice lawsuits, I have seen so many fabricated, egregious testimonies by supposed expert witnesses that are blatantly incorrect and inaccurate. They are drummed up to satisfy the plaintiff attorney's argument while getting paid handsomely for such expert testimony. Then the prosecutors will try to intimidate the defense and present a case to a lay jury that has no idea which end is up! Pray tell, how can you explain the intricacies of the medical world to a jury of nonmedical people? The venue for this event is in a courtroom where the judge and the plaintiff's attorney are golf buddies!

Clearly something is wrong with this system. Why are so many cases eventually dismissed or dropped? Why are 90 percent of those who go to trial found not guilty of malpractice? Why do we have to spend so much money, time, and effort to prosecute medical malpractice cases? Again the answer is obvious: the huge take-home fees that attorneys make on those they win.

So what are the alternatives? Read on as I discuss meaningful reform in chapter 5, but first I would like to share with you specific examples of anonymous cases I have encountered over the years and show you how stupidity, fear of malpractice suits, and lack of accountability have added to the cost of health care in our society.

Chapter 4:
Specific Examples of Anonymous Cases

Lady M

It was late on a Friday afternoon when I was on call for unassigned drop-in patients needing a surgeon. The patient in question was admitted to the family practice service, and a surgical consult was requested. The family practice team called me to assist in managing this patient's complex groin wounds, which were chronic, massively infected, and extensive, spreading down to her perineum and thighs and up to her lower abdomen.

The history I got was that this was an elderly diabetic patient who was admitted to the intensive care unit for management of an altered mental status and sepsis (serious infection with resultant serious complications that evolved in this patient involving low blood pressure, kidney failure, and multiple other system dysfunctions).

The next communication really captured my attention. "What shall we do about the maggots?" asked the intern on family practice.

"Nothing," I said. "They are nature's scavengers, eating up dead tissue for a fraction of the cost that it would take me to operatively excise or debride the same dead tissue."

Not having seen the patient yet, I headed out to the intensive care unit, dropping other tasks as I realized the urgency of the situation.

As I rounded the corner and entered the intensive care unit, I could smell the patient before I could see her. There was a nauseating smell of dead flesh and sour putrefaction wafting through the ICU. I walked into the patient's room and started getting a history from the nurse. The patient couldn't provide any information because she was paralyzed chemically and was on a ventilator with a tube down her windpipe connected to a breathing machine, making it impossible for her to talk. She was also sedated and unable to carry a conversation.

This is the information I gathered from the nursing staff: This patient was a morbidly obese diabetic who has been suffering from groin wounds for some time. She had refused evaluation by a doctor previously. When she called for her family members to help change the TV channel she was watching, they noticed that she was acting differently, with an altered mental status compared to her normal baseline, so they called 911. The patient was delivered to our hospital and admitted to a medical service. A consult for the intensive care team and the surgeon on call was requested. On my examination, I found the patient to be in a precarious state of health. She was receiving multiple drugs to support her failing blood pressure. She was getting transfused with blood products to address the bleeding problems she had developed as a result of her ongoing infection.

I rolled up my sleeves and dug in to see what I could do. I have seen a lot of pathology in my time, lots and lots of weird and advanced illnesses across the globe. Rarely do I ever feel squeamish about anything. This particular patient almost had me barfing. In between the copious skin folds around her thighs, there were gangrenous wounds that smelled horrible. There was a mountain of maggots eating away at dead and festering flesh. When I tried to explore the wounds by pulling at the skin folds, I unearthed another mountain of maggots lying underneath the folds extending down to the patient's rectum and buttocks. The process extended up to her lower abdomen and down to her perineum. Her upper thighs, front, and back were involved, and the more I dug in, the more swarming maggots I found.

Okay, let's bring Dr. Maslow back into the equation. This patient was a known diabetic who happened to suffer from high blood pressure, high cholesterol, and morbid obesity. She was bedridden and had been suffering from chronic groin wounds. The reason for her admission to the hospital was that her family was concerned about her mental status because she seemed confused while watching TV and wanted help changing the channels.

Let me ask you, should someone who was being eaten by maggots throughout the lower half of her body want to come in for medical evaluation? According to Maslow's Hierarchy of Needs, the answer is no. She was eating and pooping, warm and sheltered, so there was no need on her hierarchy of needs to seek medical care. She was eating and watching TV. Hey, who could ask for more? It was only when she seemed confused and asked for help changing the channels that her family decided to take her in!

Is this normal? Is it okay for a member of our society to go on for weeks with a smoldering groin infection on top of multiple medical problems and have maggots eating away at her dying flesh and not to come in for medical care sooner? On top of that, the reason that prompted the evaluation was that she could not change the TV channel!

What burden does this patient and her family have with regard to our health-care costs? Should she have been more diligent about trying to lose weight? Should she have been more responsible about managing her diabetes? Should she have brought her chronic groin wounds to the attention of her health-care provider before they were infested with maggots?

This patient ended up on life support, a breathing machine, a dialysis machine, and lots of drugs to support her failing circulation, in addition to lots of blood product transfusions, and eventually died from her illness. This was at a cost of hundreds of thousands of dollars to taxpayers.

The patient's sociocultural status allowed this to happen. Had she been better educated, with a family that functioned somewhat above the base of Maslow's pyramid, then she should have been able to interact with her health-care providers and participate in her wellness! But *no*, she couldn't because she and her family were at the very base of the pyramid. Despite this, they had access to medical care through CMS (Centers for Medicaid and Medicare Services), along with a gazillion other programs that I have already discussed that provide for indigent citizens. Regardless of his or her insurance status, any human being who has such a devastating problem would likely seek care regardless of ability to pay, yet this patient ignored her problem until it interfered with her ability to watch TV!

This is an example of how our society's tolerance and support of sociocultural retardation contributes to our health-care costs. This patient had the opportunity to seek medical care. She also had the support of a welfare system that allowed her to become morbidly obese. She did this right under our noses with the tacit approval of our government, which helped fund her lifestyle.

So much for involving patients in their health-care decisions. This patient had all the time in the world to participate in her health-care management, yet she chose not to. She and her family directly contributed to our health-care costs, yet they do not bear the burden of helping finance it. They had a free ticket because they are under the poverty line, so they are not accountable for anything.

The ACLU folks would argue that she had a disadvantage because she was uneducated. Sorry! No education is needed to seek medical care when your flesh is being eaten up by maggots! Again, it is the folks at the base of the pyramid who consume the most in health-care costs. There is no accountability for this. There is no governmental intervention to remedy this.

Had this patient been under the regular care of a primary care physician, with routine physicals and blood draws, she might have avoided the horrible consequences of an aggressive soft tissue infection. But that was way beyond the normal expectations and commitment levels of the patient and her family.

As long as there was a good plate of food in front of her, then anything else was secondary. Obviously there was no shortage of good food, as evidenced by her morbid obesity! Isn't it ironic that poverty and morbid obesity have a very high correlation?

Here is a typical example of how our citizens contribute to our health-care expenditure. The minorities, the underserved, the less educated, and the working poor who cannot afford health insurance are, by proportion, the biggest consumers of our health-care services.

Mr. H

Mr. H came to the emergency department complaining of pain around his anus. He was evaluated by the emergency medicine team and determined to have a *perirectal* (around the rectum) abscess. The patient was admitted to the hospitalist service (hospital-based medicine doc), who in turn called in an infectious disease consultant and a surgical consult. To his credit, the patient did have an artificial heart valve that could have become infected if the abscess were manipulated and spread bacteria through the blood stream, and he was on blood thinners for this artificial valve.

So I went see this poor guy with a painful butt. On my exam, I saw that he had a thrombosed external hemorrhoid, not a perirectal abscess. No, it's not rocket science to figure out the difference. The emergency medicine team should have known the difference, as should have the hospitalist doctor. The infectious disease doc had probably never even looked at the patient's anus. Even though the patient had an artificial heart valve, the antibiotic coverage recommendations are readily available to all medical professionals on the Internet. You simply don't need an infectious disease specialist to manage the patient.

So what ended up happening? It's simple, really. After a little bit of local anesthetic with epinephrine (to constrict blood vessels), I lanced the thrombosed hemorrhoid and evacuated the clot. Done deal, all of two minutes' work. This could have been done in the emergency room by the ER doc! Why wasn't it done then? Simple! No one wants to assume the responsibility. Pass the buck. What if something goes wrong? No one wants to get caught holding the bag. The ER passed it on to the hospitalist, who in turn passed it on the infectious diseases guy and the surgical specialist.

The other part of the equation is that a lot of MDs are not comfortable with making a diagnosis. They want corroboration from some kind of test or X-ray. The amount of time spent on training in medical school and residency has been cut down tremendously by rules and regulations that curtail the number of hours an intern or resident can work. Consequently, exposure to disease gets curtailed, and new grads are less experienced.

This happened after the famous Libby Zion case in New York where a supposedly overworked intern and resident prescribed a drug to a patient that interacted with one of her regular medications, causing a severe high fever in something known as the serotonin syndrome. This led to her death. Her father, a lawyer and contributor to the *New York Times*, publicized this and got the attention of the ACGME (Accreditation Council for Graduate Medical Education). This set forth a whole litany of work-hour regulations imposed by the authorities (Lerner, 2011).

The end result is that medical students and residents (doctors in training) are exposed to less disease than they were before. Multiple studies have shown that these work-hour restrictions have not favorably affected residents' training and more importantly, patient safety.[14] Medical errors are no fewer following the imposition of work-hour restrictions than they were before. But the consequence is that young doctors are less experienced and less exposed to disease than they were before. Any good doctor should know the difference between a thrombosed hemorrhoid and a perirectal abscess! This poor patient got admitted to the hospital, got seen by four different physicians, and incurred a bill of thousands of dollars when he could have been treated as an outpatient for a fraction of the cost.

Ms. H

Ms. H is a ninety-two-year-old nursing home resident who was brought in to our emergency department for management of hypoglycemia (low blood sugar). The lady had no complaints. The staff at the nursing home noticed that she wasn't quite herself, so they checked her blood sugar, because the patient was diabetic. They found it to be low, so she was brought to the emergency department for further treatment. That usually calls for an overall medical evaluation, a shot of sugar in the vein or sugary drink by mouth, and checking for the reason why the blood sugar dropped in the first place, all of which was done.

During the evaluation, the ER doc noticed poor Ms. H's abdomen was distended. Mind you, she had no abdominal or digestive complaints. The next order of business was the ubiquitous CAT scan. This has become the new stethoscope. Belly problems = CAT scan, chest problems = CAT scan, trauma = CAT scan head to toe. The CAT scan found the patient's large intestine to be dilated (enlarged), so at 5:00 a.m., I got a call for a surgical consult to evaluate this patient's abdomen because she was being admitted to the hospital.

The patient's abdomen was fine. Nothing surgical was going on at all. She suffered from chronic constipation, a very common condition in elderly nursing home patients. Ms. H had two previous CAT scans over the previous three months for the same reason and was evaluated

---

14   Fletcher KE, et al. Systematic review: effects of resident work hours on patient safety; Horwitz LI, et al. Changes in outcomes for internal medicine inpatients after work-hour; Volpp KG, et al. Mortality among patients in VA hospitals in the first 2 years following ACGME resident duty hour reform. *JAMA*, 2007. 298(9): 984–92; Volpp KG, et al. Mortality among hospitalized Medicare beneficiaries in the first 2 years following ACGME resident duty hour reform. *JAMA*, 2007, 298(9): 975–73.

and found not to be a surgical candidate. This information was readily available to the ED staff because all of the evaluations were done at the same facility.

This patient came in for a fairly straightforward problem that could have easily been managed as an outpatient. She got re-reevaluated for a chronic problem that had been addressed before. Her encounter that day cost thousands of dollars, used up precious resources, and added nothing to her medical care.

So the haunting question remains: why did this happen? It's simple, really. The culture of the practice of medicine has been influenced and molded into what it is today by generations of fearful and protective medicine practice. Doctors have been raked over the coals for a multitude of imaginary offenses, some not imaginary but acceptable outcomes of a less-than-perfect science. No doc wants to put his neck on the chopping block, so the innate, knee jerk reflex is to do more. You won't get castrated for doing more, but you sure as hell can if you do less. It's that simple. Never mind the fact that this patient had been evaluated for the same problem before. That was on someone else's watch, and now it was the next physician's turn to be super doc, turn over every leaf, and cover his ass from the malpractice attorneys. Such is the inbred fear of litigation that common sense and precedent are thrown out the window.

Ms. A

Ms. A is a middle-aged, obese, diabetic female who suffered from a flank abscess. It was a small abscess (boil, ball of pus) on her side. She went to see her primary care doctor, a family practice physician. She was diagnosed and then sent over to the hospital to be admitted to the hospitalist internal medicine service. An infectious disease and surgery consult were called!

Hold on one minute here. What is a family practice doc? It is a regular MD who has trained in medicine, pediatrics, obstetrics and gynecology, and surgery—the four major fields of medicine. This is someone who is very well qualified to handle the common medical issues encountered in a day-to-day family practice environment. We are not talking super specialized, complex interventions here, just bread and butter stuff.

This patient could have very easily been handled as an outpatient, had her abscess lanced at the family practice doctor's office under local anesthesia, and started on antibiotics by mouth if necessary. The medical literature would definitely support such a course of action. She had a primary care physician who was trained and capable of doing just that. But she ended up in the hospital on an internal medicine service with consults from infectious disease and surgery! A canon instead of a fly swatter. Again, the question remains, why?

Remember that medical saying, "It's easier for six people to carry a coffin than for one person"? The family practice doc didn't want to be bothered with the hassle of doing a procedure, and what if things didn't turn out well? How would it be defensible in court? It was easier to admit the patient to the hospital and consult the hospitalist. The monkey was off the family physician's back. The hospitalist followed the same logic and consulted the infectious disease specialist and the surgeon. The monkey was really bouncing around off different backs. The buck stops somewhere, though. The perpetual search is to find the highest level of specialization to pass the buck off to. That way you have better nights where you can snore away in a blissful sleep knowing that you have passed the buck on to someone higher up on the food chain and gotten rid of the monkey off your back!

The patient incurred a bill of several thousand dollars instead of a couple of hundred dollars to equivalently care for the same problem. Do you see the common thread here? Docs are scared to do the right thing. We have been conditioned to practice defensive medicine to cover our asses.

Mr. P

Mr. P is a thirty-nine-year-old ex-alcoholic who suffered from chronic pancreatitis and an obstructing pancreatic head mass. Alcoholics frequently suffer from pancreatitis, an inflammation of the pancreas gland that can lead to serious consequences. The pancreas lives in tiger country where brave surgeons tread cautiously. It is a complicated anatomical region with numerous vital structures that don't like to be messed with.

This poor guy had a chronic inflammatory mass at the head of the pancreas that caused an obstruction of the main bile duct that drains the liver's secretions and passes them through the pancreas on the way to empty into the intestine. He was being managed by the family practice service. One of the common concerns when patients have pancreatic head masses that cause obstruction is the possibility of cancer. Because of this, the primary care team ordered numerous, repetitive CAT scans with biopsies to rule out the possibility of cancer and MRIs (magnetic resonance imaging, a sophisticated radiological study), all of which were negative.

Gastrointestinal consultants were called in to temporarily stent the bile duct and relieve the obstruction. A procedure known as an ERCP (endoscopic, retrograde cholangiopancreatography) was done, where the obstructed bile duct is stented with a plastic stent to dilate it and reestablish flow through the duct. That is a great temporary measure but not a good long-term solution. The stent predictably became plugged up with secretions resulting in cholangitis, an infection in the bile duct with stagnant, infected bile. This requires a repeat ERCP with stent exchange, something the patient had done several times. All the while, the primary care team went on blissfully, hiding their heads in the sand for fear of tackling this life-threatening problem head on.

So where did I come in? I was called in to manage this patient's distended gall bladder, to perform a cholecystectomy. The gall bladder is a sac that communicates with the bile duct that drains bile from the liver, acting as a storage area for bile to be secreted into the gut when fatty foods are ingested. (Bile helps to digest fats.) The problem was that the gall bladder was dilated as a consequence of the bile duct obstruction from the pancreatic head mass. Bile backed up and filled up the gall bladder. The patient's doctors' lack of understanding of this basic plumbing led to a couple of years of endless searching for an elusive cancer that didn't exist. Regardless of whether there was a cancer or not, the treatment is the same—a Whipple procedure, which is a very complex procedure removing the head of the pancreas, the first part of the small intestine, and a portion of the stomach, with a complex reconstructive component to the procedure. It carries a high complication rate. But that's what the patient needed, plain and simple.

Instead of five or six CAT scans, MRIs, and ERCPs, endless testing, and patient discomfort over a couple of years, this poor man should have been referred for a Whipple procedure two years earlier. This treatment course cost the taxpayers hundreds of thousands of dollars. The family practice team lacked a basic understanding of this patient's pathophysiology and lacked the intestinal fortitude to grab the bull by the horns and make a definitive decision. It was something that was outside their comfort zone and could not be corroborated by endless testing.

This poor soul eventually got his Whipple procedure and did well.

Mr. AGE

Mr. AGE is a sixty-six-year-old man who presented to the emergency department with complaints of abdominal pain, nausea and vomiting, and diarrhea. The emergency medicine team proceeded with the protocol work-up, which, of course, included a CAT scan. This sophisticated X-ray was read by the radiologist as showing signs of small bowel dilatation, and therefore a small bowel obstruction could not be excluded. Consequently, the emergency department doc called in a surgical consult to rule out a small bowel obstruction (a mechanical obstruction of the intestine usually due to scar tissue from previous surgery).

That's where I came in. I went to see this patient, who was now admitted to the medical hospitalist service. Help me out here. I want you to follow along the history-taking process I used to evaluate this patient. As I teach my medical students and residents, 90 percent of the diagnosis is in a good history, and the remaining 10 percent is comprised of the physical exam (9 percent) and ancillary testing (1 percent).

"So, Mr. AGE, when did you start feeling ill?" I asked.

"Oh, Doc, it was really early this morning."

"What happened? How did it start?"

"Well, Doc, I felt a sudden cramping in my abdomen that was followed by profuse vomiting and diarrhea."

"Hum, sounds like food poisoning to me. Did you eat out anywhere yesterday?"

"Yes, Doc, as a matter of fact we went out to dinner at a restaurant that was recently rated as a poor performer on the hygienic front by one of our local news agencies."

"Did anyone else get sick?"

"Yes, Doc, my wife and friend who ate with me got sick but not as bad."

Okay, if you are a doc reading this, I have no question that you know what this is. If you're not, I still think you have a pretty darn good idea as to what this is! It's food poisoning, acute gastroenteritis (AGE). My grandmother who is not a doctor could tell you that. That's common sense. It's detective work at a very basic level. Yet this was ignored by the emergency department (ED) doc because of the inbred need to order useless tests. This patient did not need a CAT scan. A simple X-ray of the abdomen would have sufficed. The radiologist in turn, not wanting to miss anything, threw in the gamut of possible diagnoses to include small bowel obstruction, which he could not rule out because of the dilated small bowel. The ED doc in turn passed the buck on to the top of the food chain, the ultimate authority in the field—the surgeon.

This patient did not have a bowel obstruction! He and his family probably knew that. The ED doc probably did or should have known that. But that one line in the CAT scan radiologist's report about not being able to rule out a small bowel obstruction resulted in the ED doc's discomfort with assuming the responsibility of treating the patient for what was clearly a case of food poisoning. He needed a few hours in the ED with some intravenous fluid hydration and outpatient management. Yet again, he charged up a bill of thousands of dollars to treat something that could have been easily managed for much less!

Are you seeing the common thread of perpetual testing and passing the buck? I have explained this phenomenon before as fear of commitment to a diagnosis without corroborative testing and fear of assuming responsibility and the need to pass the buck on to someone else to avoid legal ramifications in case you're wrong!

Ms. I

Ms. I was an eighty-eight-year-old female who presented to the ED with complaints of severe abdominal pain, nausea and vomiting, and constipation. She had a multitude of medical problems. She was admitted to the medicine service and transferred to the intensive care unit with a consult for the critical-care medicine team to assist in her management. The poor lady stayed in the ICU for five days getting progressively worse and worse. Eventually, her kidneys shut down from dehydration, and she required dialysis. A CAT scan was ordered and revealed the patient to have dilated loops of small bowel. A surgical consult was called, and I responded.

In taking the history, I found that the patient presented with complaints of crampy, intermittent abdominal pain, associated with nausea and vomiting, constipation, and bloating. On exam, she had an obvious incarcerated (stuck) groin hernia where a loop of bowel had been caught and caused a bowel obstruction.

She went for emergency surgery, where the problem was corrected. This is not rocket science, ladies and gentlemen. This is a common diagnostic condition that should be readily identified and managed. The institution where this occurred is not in the boondocks. It is a major teaching facility with an academic affiliation. This patient was never examined properly. The emphasis on physical exam has given way to the more sophisticated diagnostic tests such as CAT scans. Had she been examined properly, the problem would have been found and the appropriate treatment initiated.

The fact that this kind of medicine can be practiced is a travesty. This poor lady almost lost her life and cost you and I hundreds of thousands of dollars when she could have been home a day after her surgery had she been diagnosed correctly when she first presented.

Ms. E

Ms. E was an elderly nursing home patient who had been in and out of the hospital for about four years with intermittent episodes of bowel obstruction. She would complain of crampy abdominal pain associated with vomiting, constipation, and bloating. She would be admitted to the hospital, and a tube would be placed through her nose into her stomach to decompress her obstructed gut. A surgical consult would be called, and the patient would be managed nonoperatively due to her advanced medical illnesses of severe rheumatoid arthritis and lots of other associated illnesses.

Her internist came to me one day and asked for a special favor. He said the patient had been admitted several times over the last few years and had been seen by almost all the surgeons at the hospital. He was at his wit's end and didn't know what to do. He asked me to see the patient and render an opinion.

"Sure," I said. "No worries, I will be happy to take a look at her." I went to see the patient and reviewed her previous workup. She had been admitted at least five times over the last couple of years and had as many CAT scans, all showing a metallic foreign body lodged on the last part of her small intestine. Curiously, no one had addressed this—not the radiologists or the surgeons evaluating this patient. The metallic X-ray effect was written off as scatter artifact from the patient's artificial hip joint, though it could not explain the location of the metallic body within the patient's small intestine.

When all else fails, go ask the patient, so I did.

"Ms. E, did you by any chance swallow a metallic object?"

"Why yes, Doc, I did. A few years ago I was evaluated by a gastroenterologist for abdominal pain. He gave me a small camera to swallow so it could take pictures of the inside of my intestines and see if there were something wrong." (This device is called a capsule enteroscope.)

"Okay, Ms. E, here you have it. You have recurrent partial small bowel obstruction from this device that got stuck in your small bowel, causing a ball valve–type of intermittent obstruction. It should have passed into the stool, but it didn't. Your symptoms and repetitive X-ray findings support the diagnosis of a partial small bowel obstruction. The only way to cure this is to take you to surgery and remove the offending device. You have a lot of medical problem and could have serious complications, but the bottom line is, unless we go after this surgically, you're not going to get better."

After a brief pause, she agreed to proceed with surgery. Surgery was successful, but did have a complicated postoperative course as expected. Eventually, the patient did well and went back to her nursing home.

What is the root cause analysis? Why did this happen? The prime reason, honestly, was the patient's complicated medical condition. She was bedridden with skeletal deformities from rheumatoid arthritis. She had a compromised healing potential from the corticosteroids she was taking for her arthritis. No one wanted to touch her with a ten-foot pole. Each surgical encounter led to a course of nonoperative management, which was temporarily successful. The surgeon in question would wash his hands and say his work was done.

No one wanted to grab the bull by the horns and deal with the problem. I believe that is why her metallic foreign body lodged in her small intestine was overlooked and attributed to something else.

Everyone was looking down the road and imagining a bad outcome because of the patient's debilitated status and got scared and intimidated for fear of legal consequences. No one would fault you for trying to be conservative in the face of a complex, medically compromised patient, but at the end of the day, the problem was not taken care of. Doctors did not do the right thing because of the inbred fear of facing potential legal ramifications of surgical complications or bad outcomes. This lady got the right treatment four years later at a cost of hundreds of thousands of dollars to you and me from multiple hospital admissions, CAT scans, and surgical consults.

Mr. Celiac Axis Stenosis

The medical intern called me to evaluate a patient with abdominal pain. I was being consulted to see if I could offer a solution to this patient's arterial insufficiency to his gut. The story goes as follows.

Mr. Celiac Axis Stenosis was an elderly man who presented to the doctor with a few weeks' history of diffuse lower abdominal pain that was constant and dull in nature. He also had constant nausea and anorexia. He was surviving on sips of liquids because he had no desire to eat any substantial meals. He was also suffering from intermittent high fevers.

He had been admitted to the hospital four times in the last few weeks. The working diagnosis was diverticulitis, an infection in the lower part of the large intestine. This diagnosis was reached because his pain was in the lower abdomen, he had a slight elevation in his white blood cell count, indicating an infection, and the ubiquitous CAT scan was read by the radiologist as "cannot exclude early diverticulitis," which is a cover-your-ass, generic statement to pass the diagnostic buck back to the clinician.

I looked at the patient's CAT scan and saw absolutely no evidence of diverticulitis. Diverticulitis did not explain his several-week history of nausea, vague diffuse lower abdominal pain, and anorexia despite several courses of antibiotics. In their ever-expanding search for a diagnosis, the medical team requested a CT angiogram, which is a highly specialized CAT scan looking at the blood supply of the intestine, thinking that the cause of the problem just might be something called *mesenteric angina* or *mesenteric ischemia*, a shortage of blood supply to the gut. Well, lo and behold, the CT angiogram revealed a narrowing in the main artery that supplies the upper gut with blood. Feeling vindicated, the clueless medical docs waved that result in our faces, demanding a surgical intervention to terminate their poor patient's suffering.

Never mind that mesenteric angina or ischemia does not present in this way. Never mind that people have alternate blood supply (three main sources) to their gut and that if one or two of these are open, the narrowing or occlusion of one is readily tolerated.

The patient had a multitude of tests that did not corroborate the medical doctors' initial diagnostic impression of mesenteric angina. He had an *esophagogastroduodenoscopy*, which is where a fancy, flexible camera goes down the gullet into the stomach and first part of the small intestine, which was unremarkable, something totally unlikely with a diagnosis of mesenteric ischemia in that setting. He had a CAT scan, a CT angiogram, a multitude of blood tests, a few specialist consults, and a trip to the intensive care unit.

Mesenteric angina presents with a main history of feeding avoidance. It is like having angina of the gut instead of the heart. When the blood supply to the gut is compromised and a patient increases the demand on the blood supply by eating, the gut develops a deficiency in its blood supply compared to its baseline fasting state, causing significant pain with food. This is a prolonged process leading to feeding avoidance and a thin patient. That was not the story here. Mesenteric ischemia is an exaggerated process of blood starvation, where the gut is literally dying because of lack of blood supply (a gut attack, if you will). Both those conditions could be easily excluded from this patient's differential diagnosis based on clinical grounds.

The patient had constant lower abdominal pain, not episodic pain in relation to meals. He was nauseated and anorexic throughout. He had been suffering with this problem for several weeks, an unlikely event in mesenteric ischemia, where he should have deteriorated in days, and he had an endoscopy revealing no evidence of ischemia. He suffered from intermittent fevers as well, suggesting an alternate etiology. To appease the medical doctors and prove to them that this patient did not have diverticulitis or mesenteric ischemia, and to exclude any surgical etiology for this patient's problem, I decided to perform a simple diagnostic test by performing an exploratory laparoscopy. This is a procedure in which a small camera is inserted into the abdomen and used to explore the abdominal contents with the aid of a couple of small incisions through which instruments can be inserted to manipulate the abdominal contents, a minimally invasive procedure with few, if any, drawbacks and maximal information.

As predicted, the exploration was totally normal. I presented this fact to the medical team, and much to my surprise, they were undeterred in their misguided belief that because there was evidence of narrowing of an artery, that must be the cause of this patient's troubles. Never mind that his symptoms and clinical findings, his extensive tests and workups, his negative endoscopy, and surgical exploration all threw that diagnosis into the trash can. They were not deterred. There was objective evidence of an abnormal fancy test, so therefore, that must be where the problem lies. This patient was another victim of modern imaging technology (VOMIT).

They were barking up the wrong tree, no ifs, ands, or buts. Their next step? They called in an interventional cardiologist to open up that artery by ballooning and stenting it. The poor guy was intimidated into treating this patient. After many disclaimer statements about how he did not think this treatment was going to help the patient, he went in to dilate the artery in question to improve the blood supply.

The result? There was no difference! The same problem existed. The work-up is still in progress. The message I am delivering here is that we will relentlessly pursue a diagnosis through whatever means we have at our disposal without thought of its likelihood or consequence. Gone are the days of clinical acumen, the days of diagnostic accuracy. Our new generation relies on a plethora of tests and fancy X-rays to reach a diagnosis. They have no vested interest in the clinical aspects of disease—only things they can prove with CAT scans, MRIs, blood tests, and so on.

The system incurred the cost of unnecessary X-rays and procedures, all to appease the insatiable curiosity and medico-legal paranoia of the primary medical team. It was a case of mental masturbation once again. While subjecting this patient to unnecessary tests and exposing him to risks of unnecessary procedures, they were bankrupting our health-care system in the process.

When I signed off the case for lack of surgical issues, the diagnosis was still being pursued.

Ms. Necrotizing Fasciitis

A morbidly obese, diabetic patient was admitted by the family practice service to the intensive care unit because of out-of-control diabetes, something known as DKA (diabetic ketoacidosis), a condition in which diabetic patients suffer from a serious elevation in their blood sugar and a resultant derangement in their bodies' metabolism, frequently brought on by a serious infection.

This poor patient was on prescribed diabetic medication, which she was not taking because they were too expensive, and she ran out of meds. Her blood sugar gradually climbed up to a dangerously high level, and her metabolism shut down, causing her to get seriously ill and present to the emergency department. She was diagnosed and admitted to the intensive care unit. Her primary care team was notified so they could take care of her.

The patient had an elevation of her liver function tests, which is not an uncommon problem when patients are *septic*—suffering from a serious infection. The primary care team went on a witch hunt in search of a gall bladder problem because that can also present with elevated liver enzymes on the blood work. Yup, you guessed it—a CAT scan was ordered. Ahhh, the patient had already had her gall bladder removed! On the CAT scan, it was noted that the patient had air bubbles underneath her abdominal *pannus*—the fatty apron that hangs down over the lower abdomen of a morbidly obese patient. The primary care team had noticed skin lesions that were described as vesicles (fluid-filled sacs) over the pannus, for which they had called in a dermatologist to rule out shingles! Shingles can present as vesicles, but nothing like this.

When I was finally called in a few days later, I saw a patient on death's door. She had *necrotizing fasciitis*—a flesh-eating bacterial infection that is often lethal. I took her to the operating room several times for debridement of the dead tissue and eventually removed the majority of her anterior abdominal wall and reconstructed it with skin grafts from other parts of her body.

The cost drivers in this case are numerous. The patient's morbid obesity definitely played a part. She was from a lower socioeconomic sector of society and of Hispanic ethnicity, both factors being associated with a higher rate of morbid obesity. Our failed health-care system that allowed a patient to go without medicines because she could not afford them was also responsible. The meds could have been subsidized at cost and helped save the hundreds of thousands of dollars the government (you and I) dished out eventually to pay for her lengthy, costly hospitalization. The mental masturbation and lack of experience of the primary health-care team delayed the diagnosis and treatment of this patient. The appearance of violaceous discoloration and vesicles on the skin of her pannus in her clinical setting of diabetic ketoacidosis is a dead giveaway for necrotizing fasciitis, but that wasn't enough. A dermatologist was called in to rule out shingles by aspirating the fluid from the bubbles and testing it. Another CAT scan was ordered to evaluate her further, and that's when the air bubbles were noticed and a surgery consult called. She didn't need a dermatology consult. She didn't need a CAT scan. What she needed was a responsive health-care system that should have provided her with diabetic medication and a health-care team that didn't procrastinate in reaching a diagnosis by ordering tests ad nauseam.

This is bad medicine. It should not exist. Yet it is the status quo in our country, and it's only getting worse. I think you get the message from the multiple examples I have highlighted above. Whether the blame falls on the patient, the doctor, or the legal system, the cost of health-care delivery is rising exponentially out of control. All these factors contribute to the cost of health care. By giving you concrete, anonymous examples, I hope to have shared with you candid scenarios garnished from my daily experiences about how medicine is practiced in this country. This is not meant to be an exhaustive list of all the medical mishaps that occur but rather a diversified case log offered as educational examples to the lay public, who may not otherwise know the truth about the intricacies of the practice of medicine. Again, this is an effort to shed light on cost drivers, and it is not intended to embarrass or belittle my colleagues. These things do happen, as embarrassing as they may be. They have to be acknowledged and their root cause analysis undertaken.

Chapter 5: Meaningful Reform

In chapter 1, I gave you an understanding of how our medical and health insurance systems work. In chapter 2, I gave you an analysis of how our system compares to the rest of the world. In chapter 3, I discussed the impact of specific health-care cost drivers, and in chapter 4, I gave you anonymous and concrete examples of how the medical profession can contribute to the tremendous cost of health care.

Now, in chapter 5, I will share with you my thoughts on meaningful reform. Our system is broken and rapidly spiraling into a black hole. Our government's financial reserves are nonexistent. We have unprecedented debt. Health-care costs are skyrocketing out of control. Medicaid and Medicare services are nearly bankrupt. Financial reimbursement to health-care providers continues to decrease as the consumer price index continues to increase and the cost of doing business along with it. Our malpractice environment is adding to the cost of health care without question and tainting the environment in which we practice. Numerous encounters generate a sense of angst in the heart of the health-care provider as he or she contemplates the lip-smacking, drooling trial attorney waiting to take him or her to the cleaners. Resources are wasted on covering one's ass to make sure nothing bad can happen and no stone is left unturned. Consultants are called in, and the patient and family are coddled to avoid any risk of litigation. The traditional doctor-patient relationship of mutual respect, trust, and appreciation is frequently turned into a contractual agreement.

This status quo needs more than fine tuning. It needs to be put in a plastic bag, turned upside down, and shaken out of its miserable existence. We need a clean slate to reestablish a health-care system that can work—that we can afford and be proud of. As I stated earlier, no meaningful reform is going to come without sacrifice and sacrifice along several fronts at that.

The world's most economically prolific country cannot have uninsured citizens! It is a travesty. Other less economically fortunate countries have managed to implement universal health care for their citizens and so should we. I say to the naysayers, don't tell me that their systems are inferior to ours and that we have the best system in the world. I'm sorry, but that's just not true! Please refer to the comparative analysis of different health-care delivery models in chapter 2. The analysis clearly shows that our system is not the best in the world. Medical tourism in countries like India delivers excellent, if not better, results at a fraction of the costs incurred in the United States. The legal catalyst of medical malpractice is eliminated so the system can function in a truly free economic model.

The United Declaration of Human Rights and the World Health Organization's position on universal health-care coverage needs to be adopted, emulated, and implemented. How we do this is a subject of debate. In this chapter, I will systematically tackle the issues at hand that are preventing us from achieving this goal. I will offer constructive arguments on meaningful reform that will positively impact our health-care environment. These are not going to be baby steps. These arguments are surgically oriented approaches designed to extirpate the cancer that is eating away at our society. We will not achieve any significant change if we continue to debate minutiae and offer sheaves of bureaucratic government legal documents that no one can understand, digest, or remember. We need simple, understandable solutions that can be implemented.

Integrated Medical Group Practice

First on my chopping block is the way medicine is practiced in the United States. The mom-and-pop cottage industry model that has prevailed over the years is a dinosaur. It is no secret that integrated group practice models such as the Mayo Clinic, Scott and White, Kaiser Permanente, and Marshfield Clinic, to name a few, offer comprehensive medical care for less money with better outcomes. The government has been trying to push us toward this model as far back as 1932 (US government Committee on the Cost of Medicine).

American medicine tends to be very fragmented. This has a lot to do with the geography of the medical home. The medical home is not a geographically linked structure or a multilevel, large building housing the entire medical team. Rather, it is a small village of individual, unconnected, smaller buildings individually housing the various members of the medical team. This makes information sharing and strategic planning more difficult to accomplish. Each medical practitioner sees the patient from a particular viewpoint pertaining to his or her specialty.

In addition, there is the compelling need for multiple specialists to be involved in the patient's care to satisfy the medico-legal paranoia that permeates the very fabric of the practice of medicine today. Each physician may be blinded as to what the other members of the patient's care team are doing or what studies have been ordered for the patient.

Large, integrated organizations have economies of scale. They have a common medical record. They have the ability to negotiate from a stronger position because of their volume. It is easier for an organization that is integrated and marching to the beat of a single drummer to make changes, implement positive practice characteristics, and track performance parameters, resource utilization, and adherence to evidence-based medicine. The mass and financial clout of such a large, integrated organization allows for integration of health-care delivery across the entire patient-care spectrum. Outpatient and inpatient care, home health services, and nursing home and hospice services can all be integrated.

Mom-and-pop practices have no cohesion. They have no economies of scale. They answer to no one. There is no commonality. Each practice has its own type of electronic medical record or even an outdated paper record. There is no data sharing and no statistical trending. There are no practice outcome measures. There is no accountability. Trying to get independent doctors to work together is like trying to herd cats. Physicians are notoriously independent and opinionated beings. It's my way or the highway.

An integrated medical group practice can offer all these advantages. A patient can have a medical home, where there is transparency of the medical record. Repetitive tests are not necessary because they are readily available for all to see once they have been done. Physician reimbursement is not dependent on the extent of service rendered or amount of tests ordered but on a competitive salary with a performance incentivization bonus structure. Do your job well and get compensated well. Do your job exceptionally well and deliver comparable or superior outcomes for fewer health-care costs and get compensated even better.

Group purchasing decisions and inventory supply-chain management can be an organization-wide practice rather than the fragmented status of free-standing practices and hospitals. Dr. A likes this kind of glove, gown, implant, and mesh while Dr. B doesn't, so we stock everything to please everyone—meanwhile losing economies of scale attained by large group purchasing agreements. Doctors have to come to an agreement with some sacrifice regarding which standardized equipment, implants, etc., are going to be utilized across the organization. For the most part, once they are shown the cost savings of certain purchasing decisions, the majority will play along nicely.

Integrated medical group practices have the ability to negotiate purchasing contracts with vendors for the whole organization, thus taking out the individual physician from the equation. The organization has made a decision to use this drug instead of this drug because it is half the cost and has comparable results to other drugs in its class. Similarly, we will be using this particular implant for hip joints for similar reasons. Of course, these decisions will be made by the administrative body in conjunction with input from physicians, but the final decision will be free of financial kickbacks—transparent and accountable.

Rather than paying individual providers separately for their services, bundled payment is already being considered by the Centers for Medicare & Medicaid Services. Fees will be bundled together for a single disease diagnosis, leaving the providers to fight among themselves for the spoils. This proposed payment model is very different from the current one that was described in chapter 1. In the future model, recipients are coalesced together as one recipient. A patient who is treated for appendicitis will have a lump sum paid to a single entity, and all the separate physicians involved in treating the patient will have to negotiate their share with that entity (emergency medicine doctor, surgeon, anesthesiologist, radiologist, pathologist, etc.).

These fees will also be reduced and subject to modification based on quality outcomes. If a patient suffers a preventable complication during a treatment program, the cost of treatment for that complication will not be reimbursed. For example, if a patient gets admitted for a surgical procedure and ends up getting a surgical wound infection, a urinary tract infection, pneumonia, or any other recognized potential complication, the cost of treating that complication will not be reimbursed. That's the government's solution to saving money.

It's one thing to track and benchmark outcome statistics and a completely different thing to hide one's head in the sand and assume that "acts of God" should not happen. Complications are a way of life. No matter how good the surgeon or the institution, complications will happen. If you swipe the butts of a hundred people with an alcohol swab and give them an intramuscular injection, a few of them will get an infection, regardless of how skilled you are as an injectionist. That's a matter of fact. Similarly, regardless of how stringently you follow current guidelines, infections will happen. Yet, the government is penalizing the medical industry for unavoidable outcomes. I understand if your infection rate is way over the acceptable benchmark, but if you are doing a good job and end up with an unavoidable outcome, you should not be penalized for it. It has nothing to do with appropriate medical care and everything to do with finances. The government is running out of money, plain and simple. They have to cut back somewhere, so an easy excuse is to punish any deviation from the gold standard of perfection.

Future Health-Care Model

- Integrated, coordinated service across an organization
- Bundled payment for multiple providers
- Quality and efficiency rewarded
- Cohesion among practitioners
- Economics of scale
- Incentive to spend less and provide better results

This is not a reasonable course of action. It is the demonstration of the final death throes of a failing system trying desperately to conserve resources. Unfortunately, they are barking up the wrong tree. That's not how you save money. That's how you alienate people and decrease the desire of college graduates to enter the medical profession.

Whatever Medicare and Medicaid implement is sure to be followed by the rest of the insurance industry, so this is going to be the new insurance paradigm. Gone will be the old ways of fee-for-service.

Practitioners will now have to bargain with hospitals and other health-care providers to divvy up the goodies. This will force fragmented sectors to collaborate and join forces. Mind you, this is not part of my reform plan; it's just the face of things to come. In response, we have to be proactive and organize ourselves accordingly. We either remain solo, individual practitioners, trying to get the lion's share of the goodies, or become an organized group working together to achieve economic advantage with equitable distribution of proceeds. By reducing our overhead, minimizing the cost of health-care delivery, and achieving quality results that are benchmarked against posted standards, we can continue to enjoy a positive cash flow for the organization, from which we can all benefit.

Medical Sales and Pharmaceuticals

Medical sales are a multibillion-dollar industry. Medical products are expensive. Granted, some deserve to be expensive because they require years of research and development, production, and marketing costs that need to be recouped by the developer. But let's be reasonable. According to livestrong.com, *Insight Journal* reports that many of the active ingredients in prescription drugs are manufactured overseas and that the pharmaceutical industry earns from 2,809 percent markup of the cost of active ingredient in Zestril to as much as 570,000 percent markup in Xanax. The markup for Xanax is based on a consumer price of $137.79 for one hundred tablets and $0.024 for the cost of the active ingredients. (Read more at http://www.livestrong.com/article260599-prescription-drug-cost-vs-sale-price/#ixzz1wflXVqKS.)

Medical product sales reps are notoriously cute, sexy ladies or handsome hunks of men. This is no coincidence, nor are the "educational dinners and trips" the companies provide free of charge to help bring the latest and greatest products to your attention. Then there are the fully paid Las Vegas trips where you get to spend a day at a training institute pushing that company's particular product and then party like it's 1964 at the expense of the company.

Mind you, I'm not saying that these are not good products. I'm just saying there should be an ethical and meritorious way to make purchasing decisions other than how short was the rep's skirt was and how much money she spent on my dinner.

Some of the products I use in the operating room are very similar to the products I keep in the tool box in my garage. A nail is a nail, whether it is titanium or steel. Sure, one costs more, but it is a freaking nail, not a complicated scientific instrument. Most of the hardware used in orthopedic surgery (bones) can be bought off the shelf at Sears with minor modifications and put to work for a fraction of the cost of what the manufacturer charges. If you were to compare the cost of a hip replacement in the United States versus other countries, you would see that the same product costs a whole lot less, while being done by comparable surgeons in American-accredited hospitals in these foreign countries that are accredited by the Joint Commission on Accreditation of Hospitals. According to medicaltourism.com, hip replacement surgery in India, Costa Rica, and Mexico breaks down as follows:

> Total Hip Replacement Package Price: 7,000 to 15,000 US Dollars covering all the medical & logistic costs at the destination in Costa Rica [USA Joint Commission International-Accredited Hospital], India [Harvard Medical-Affiliated & USA Joint Commission-Accredited Hospital] and Mexico [World Class Hospitals].

The cost of a total hip replacement in the United States varies depending upon where it is performed. As per costhelper.com, for patients without health insurance, a total hip replacement usually will cost between $31,839 and $44,816, with an average cost of $39,299, according to Blue Cross Blue Shield of North Carolina.

These surgeries are performed by the best hip replacement doctors that have experience of several successful hip replacement procedures. Many of the doctors have worked in the United States or Europe. I wonder why the costs are so much higher in the United States. Could it have anything to do with legal cost markup or business practices that are uncontested?

The United States is the only country in the world where drug prices are not regulated by the government, and along with New Zealand, the only country where advertising pharmaceutical drugs directly to consumers is practiced. Officially, it is illegal to purchase prescription drugs outside of the United States. The FDA's stand is that they cannot guarantee the quality of these drugs, though some of these US-standardized drugs come from the very same countries they are calling unreliable. The high cost of prescription drugs and the high number of uninsured in need of such drugs have generated significant interest in foreign drugs. The recent escalation in narcotic drug–related violence in Mexico has drastically limited the number of patients crossing our southern border for their prescriptions, but Canada is a prime shopping spot.[15]

Though it is illegal to purchase foreign prescription drugs, the government will turn a blind eye and allow for a three-month personal supply to cross the border. In fact, the congressional budget office estimated that allowing Medicare and Medicaid to purchase drugs from Canada and other selected countries would save taxpayers over $19 billion. Legislation to legalize drug importation has been signed into law by Bill Clinton and George W. Bush but never went into effect because their respective health secretaries refused to guarantee the safety of the drugs as the laws required (AARP). Obviously Barrack Obama is trying to do the same.

The pharmaceutical business is just that, a business, and like all publically traded companies, its prime responsibility is to satisfy its shareholders by maximizing profits. That's how capitalism works—encouraging innovation and risk taking. That's how it works in the United States and in the rest of the world. The difference is that in the United States, the cost of a drug for the pharmacist to sell and hence for the patient to buy is the highest in the world. In fact, the current average profit margin for the drug manufacturing industry is 16 percent, with most of the major drug companies seeing profits well over 20 percent (Yahoo! Finance). Drug companies claim that the high cost of prescription drugs is due to expensive research and development costs. However, Dr. Donald Light of the University of Medicine and Dentistry of New Jersey and economist Rebecca Warburton of the University of Victoria claim that pharmaceutical companies greatly exaggerate their research and development (R&D) expenditures, that costs are "unknown and highly variable," and that 84.2 percent of all funds used by pharmaceutical companies for R&D come from public sources (Light & Warburton, 2011).

---

15 Barry, Patricia, "More Americans Go North for Drugs," *AARP Bulletin*, April 2003; Millman, Joel, "Not Your Generic Smugglers—American Seniors Flock to Border Town for Cheap Prescriptions," *Wall Street Journal*, March 20, 2003; Pringle, Paul, "Not-So Corner Drugstore; Canadian Web Firms Are Supplying Low-Cost Prescriptions to Many Elderly Americans. But Manufacturers and Regulators Are Chafing," *Los Angeles Times*, February 21, 2003.

Health-Care Reform: A Surgeon's Perspective

In her 2003 book, *The Big Fix: How the Pharmaceutical Industry Rips Off American Consumers,* author Katharine Greider presents the cost breakdown of Lipitor—a $100 pill commonly prescribed for high cholesterol. The cost breakdown is as follows: 15 percent research and development, 24 percent profit, 26 percent other, including CEO pay, and 35 percent marketing. She goes on to state that in the 1999–2000 election cycle, drug companies spent more money to influence politicians than did insurance companies, telephone companies, electric companies, commercial banks, oil and gas producers, automakers, tobacco companies, and food processors and manufacturers. They spent more, in short, than any other industry (Greider, 2003). Jim Drinkard, writing for *USA Today* in an article published on April 25, 2005, found that since 1998, drug companies had spent $758 million on lobbying—more than any other industry, according to government records analyzed by the Center for Public Integrity, a watchdog group. He also found that in Washington, the industry has 1,274 lobbyists—more than two for every member of Congress.

Profit margins are unregulated, with no MSRP. Countries that have nationalized health care have a much lower cost of drug to the pharmacist and to the patient by allowing for large group purchasing. Their pharmaceutical industries are thriving, not going belly up. Other countries with non-single-payer systems regulate the sales prices of pharmaceutical drugs. The pharmaceutical industry in the United States enjoys one of the highest profit margins of any industry. Granted, R&D costs money, but the profit margin is over and above R&D expenses. Some R&D endeavors are minor modifications on already-existing patented drugs, with very little effort, design, or innovation going into the research and development. This is exemplified by all the statin drugs, a group of cholesterol-lowering drugs that have nearly identical molecular structures. Since the statute of limitations is about to expire, a "me-too" sister drug has been researched and developed with very minimal effort because the modifications are slight. However, the pharmaceutical company gains several more years of patent rights before its generic equivalent can be sold for a fraction of the price.

It's time for the federal government to jump in and regulate the medical supply and pharmaceutical industries. I'm not suggesting that we eliminate our capitalist business model—not at all. Healthy profits are good for the company, its shareholders, and the public at large. But when this unbridled greed affects our citizens' health and our country's financial viability, then it is the duty of the government to take action and put the brakes on. I wish I had the answer as to how the government should regulate pricing, but I don't. I do know, however, that it needs to be done. A task force can investigate this matter and see how countries like Canada and others are doing it.

Mental Masturbation

This has to come to a stop! I have shown you in chapter 3 how unnecessary, wasteful testing to rule out the rarest of zebra diagnoses and prove without a shadow of a doubt that doctors' clinical diagnoses are supported by some fancy test or X-ray drives up health-care costs. I have supported this with specific cases as concrete examples in chapter 4. Simply identifying the common cause of a particular clinical condition with basic history taking, physical exam skills, and a few ancillary tests being ordered just isn't very "sexy," as we say in medicine. It's mundane, boring, and not very intellectually stimulating. But let's face it, common things are common, and uncommon manifestations of common things are more common than common manifestations of uncommon things.

The thrill in medicine is to conjure up the rarest of diseases that might present in the way a particular patient is presenting and to pursue its workup with a vengeance. Then our diagnostic skills are challenged, and we can have long and erudite discussions about the differential diagnosis of this patient's symptoms and signs and the tests needed to identify the correct disease and its best treatment option. Again we must think about the horses and zebras issue when one hears hoofbeats.

We are trying to emphasize to our students that they should not miss rarer forms of disease, which is absolutely fine, but we have to keep it in context. We cannot throw common sense and clinical acumen by the wayside and hang on to each and every word that is generated in a CAT scan report because the radiologist makes a blanket statement to cover his ass that states he cannot rule out a bowel obstruction in the appropriate clinical setting. Everyone knows or should know that a patient with gastroenteritis does not have a bowel obstruction. It is a clinical diagnosis. X-ray investigation used to be limited to simple, plain X-rays of the abdomen, but now the CAT scan has become the gold standard. The gold standard of the radiologist's read of a CAT scan is, "Cannot rule out an early bowel obstruction or early appendicitis in the appropriate clinical setting." This prompts the clinician to correlate clinically, taking the monkey off his back. The ordering doc will call in a surgeon, and the monkey is now off his back! This surgeon is the ultimate authority on abdominal pathology, so he puts the matter to rest.

Not only is this type of practice unnecessary, but it is also unsustainable and dangerous because it subjects patients to repetitive, unnecessary testing, which in and of itself picks up certain false positive results that generate another cycle of further testing. Some of these interventions carry a certain amount of risk and can contribute to complications. Unfortunately, this practice pattern is tied in to the medical malpractice paranoia that fuels it, so we will not get rid of one without the other. But there are still some measures that can be adopted to tackle this growing monster.

Economic Credentialing

Physicians—especially surgeons and particularly sub-specialty surgeons (cardiothoracic, orthopedic, transplant, and so on)—are very opinionated creatures. Domineering, self-reliant, autonomous personalities are drawn to these specialties. The autonomy, self-reliance, and ultimate say in the management of patients drive this personality type. This type of doctor is used to having his way. He doesn't have to answer to anyone—but money talks.

What is the cost of practicing medicine for this particular individual? How do his patients fare? How many visits a year does he offer his patients? How easy is it to get an initial or follow-up appointment with him? What kind of routine screening tests does he order? Does he keep up with the published, benchmarked criteria for annual screening studies? What is his readmission rate compared to his peers when they are taking care of the same illness? What are his operative complication rates and his patients' average length of hospital stay? How does he compare to his peers? How much does he cost the system to treat disease X as benchmarked with his colleagues?

These are all very valid and loaded questions that can clearly demonstrate outlying physicians compared to their peers. If Dr. A can deliver the same or better quality of care for less money than Dr. B, then Dr. A should be rewarded accordingly. If I cost the system twice as much to treat a patient with appendicitis as my colleague, then I should be punished for that by collecting less for the same service and counseled on how to emulate the best-practice guidelines that my colleague is adhering to. A practice score card, if you will, should be kept on each physician and reviewed with him periodically. Best practice medicine guidelines should be encouraged, and deviation from them should be disincentivized. This paradigm should not stop at the institution's geographic walls. It should be a transparent statistic that should be shared with all facilities and used to help standardize health-care pathways to minimize regional geographic patterns that offer different levels of health care to patients suffering from similar illnesses with similar demographics to ensure similar outcomes with similar resources.

Real Evidence-Based Medicine

The medical profession needs to be held accountable for the kind of medicine being practiced. There are numerous government-approved published guidelines and protocols for the management of various diseases, like congestive heart failure, pneumonia, and heart attack, for example. We are held accountable for our treatment of these illnesses. But what happens when a medical intern consults me to take care of an infected below-the-knee amputation stump and has ordered a CAT scan to prove his case? Nothing happens. I don't need a freaking CAT scan to diagnose an infected surgical incision. It adds nothing and alters nothing in the course of care, yet he has no accountability and neither does his supervising attending.

Likewise, a twelve-year-old girl who comes into the ER with classic appendicitis doesn't need a CAT scan either. However, you can rest assured that she's going to get one. Patients who are exposed to repetitive radiation have a higher risk of getting cancer in the future, but this won't enter into the decision-making equation because a CAT scan is now a fairly standard investigation for patients with abdominal pain, though there is no convincing scientific evidence to prove that patients treated in this way fare any better than patients who are treated by selective scanning based on the assessment of the consulting surgeon. Again, there are no consequences to this practice style, and if anything, it may be encouraged because it helps ward off the evil lawyers.

Limiting Privileges

A tougher but effective method of curtailing useless testing is to allow fewer people to be able to order higher-level tests. The zealous intern cannot order a CAT scan unless he gets approval from his supervising attending, who in turn needs to follow practice guidelines and be held accountable for his or her use of technology. Similarly, higher-order tests and X-rays should be limited to the order of the consulting specialist. Belly pain in the ER? Got questions about the case? Call the surgeon. Run it by him or her, and see if he or she thinks it's a good idea. After all, the surgeon is the most qualified doctor to render an opinion about abdominal pain. The proverbial buck stops with the surgeon.

Meaningful Tort Reform

By tort reform, I don't mean caps on noneconomic damages; I mean radical tort reform. As a practicing physician, I can tell you without a shadow of a doubt that our malpractice environment radically escalates health-care costs. Cover-your-ass medicine is the standard of care. Each and every physician is looking over his shoulder during every patient encounter. A lot of what is done is done to satisfy a jury. The train of thought and logic always contains the eventuality of a lawsuit, so the doc talks to the jury through the medical record. "See what a good doc I am. I ordered every test I could and called in every consultant I needed to take care of this dear patient. I didn't leave a stone unturned, so the bad outcome was not my fault."

Doctors ordering doing unnecessary tests to prevent a lawsuit is a difficult fact to prove. There are few published studies that can document the amount of defensive medicine that is being practiced; it is difficult to quantify. A physician responding to a questionnaire might very well answer differently if the questions were being asked by his specialty board examiner regarding the best treatment strategy for a particular patient versus questions from a journalist or a surveyor about the amount of defensive medicine he practices. The answers to such questions will obviously differ based on the malpractice environment the doctor practices in, which is markedly different from state to state and from county to county. But there have been a few studies. According to Miller, 20 percent of all orthopedic imaging studies were done for defensive medicine purposes, accounting for 35 percent of the cost of care.[16]

According to Paul Manner, MD, though defensive medicine is obviously prevalent, the exact amount practiced is surprisingly hard to define. He did, however, identify a number of authors who generated hard numbers regarding the practice of defensive medicine. A survey

---

16 Miller R, et al. "The prevalence of defensive orthopaedic imaging: A spective practice audit in Pennsylvania," *AAOS* 2011; Abstract 119.

of three hundred physicians, one hundred nurses, and one hundred hospital administrators found that 79 percent of physicians ordered more tests than they thought were necessary, and 91 percent observed other physicians ordering unnecessary tests. According to the study, 74 percent of physicians ordered specialty consultations they did not think were necessary and 51 percent ordered invasive procedures, such as biopsies, that they did not think were necessary. Doctors also reported that they had observed 73 percent of other physicians ordering antibiotics that they thought were unnecessary, and 41 percent had reported doing it themselves.

Similarly, 66 percent of nurses and 84 percent of hospital administrators felt that unnecessary or excessive care was being provided for fear of malpractice litigation. He also found that the fear of medical malpractice litigation resulted in more diagnostic testing and more hospital admissions by emergency department physicians without any difference in outcome for the patients whether they were admitted to the hospital or not. A survey of eight hundred physicians in Pennsylvania found that 93 percent practiced defensive medicine, while 42 percent of respondents reported that they avoided patients who were likely to lead to a malpractice situation, such as complex patients, high-risk patients, trauma patients, and patients who were perceived as litigious.[17]

A case in point is when patients in the intensive care unit are sedated to allow them to tolerate being on a breathing machine and undergoing various painful procedures; they frequently take a few days to recover from their sedation after it is turned off. That is the norm. It is a result of drug build-up over days or weeks, storage in their body, and release after it is discontinued. It is known as ICU psychosis or delirium. Each and every time this happens, the patient is subjected to a CAT scan of the head to make sure there isn't a problem, such as a bleed in the head or a stroke, and every single time in my long career the results have always been negative! These are totally unnecessary tests unless there are some other neurological findings to support the concern, but they will continue to be done for fear of missing that one-in-a-few-million diagnosis that might present that way and to avoid getting ripped a new one by the plaintiff's attorney.[18]

The American College of Surgeons has guidelines for the evaluation of trauma patients that are universally distributed through residency

---

17   Jan/Feb 2007, AAOS. Now http://www.aaos.org/news/bulletin/janfeb07

18   Jay S Balachandran, http://www.biomedcentral.com/1471-2253/9/3.

programs and through tutorial seminars certifying physicians in the practice of trauma medicine through the Advanced Trauma Life Support program (ATLS) that is offered through the college. The recommendations for X-ray evaluation are for an X-ray of the neck spine, chest, and pelvis to be performed if the mechanism of trauma warrants the concern. The recommendations call for an X-ray, not a CAT scan. It's the difference between a snapshot and an HD movie. One can get a CAT scan as the workup progresses and if there is an indication for a CAT scan. At the institution where I work, the standard protocol for a trauma patient workup is a CAT scan of the head, neck, chest, abdomen, and pelvis! Why? I don't know! I guess they feel more secure and comfortable about covering their bases. If an X-ray is good, a CAT scan is better, so no one can mess with us if we CT this guy from head to toe. We have irrefutable evidence on our side.

I think it would help for the reader to understand that this is done without any financial consideration on the part of the hospital. The hospital is not making more money by doing CAT scans on trauma patients; quite the contrary. For one, a large percentage of our trauma patients are uninsured and can't afford to pay out of pocket. Those patients who do have insurance are subject to DRGs (diagnosis-related group), which is a payment system that was developed by Yale management and public health scholars in the '80s to bundle payment to hospitals based on the product provided. For example, a patient gets an appendectomy; a value is assigned to that product based on the patient's age, gender, medical condition, and so on. The hospital gets paid a lump sum and does not get to charge for each and every aspect of care by itemizing the bill. Because of this, it actually is in the hospital's interest to do less rather than more. That is what our malpractice environment has done to us. We have become pathologically paranoid.

I think you get the picture. This process takes a toll on the practice of medicine and the patient/physician relationship. The fact that medical malpractice is such a prevalent part of our society has influenced the traditional relationship between doctor and patient. One of my patients had a blockage of the main artery that supplied his leg with blood. He needed a bypass to reestablish the blood supply to the leg. In my discussion with the patient and his wife about the procedure, I went over the usual discussion of possible risks and complications, including the fact that the new bypass might not last forever and the patient might need to have an intervention to deal with problems down the road.

The wife asked me why that was so. I thought that was a reasonable question. I explained that her husband's God-given anatomy had failed because of hardening of his arteries—atherosclerosis—which was affected by genetics, diet, and lifestyle choices (smoking). The new anatomy I would create would be in an attempt to help fix his initial problem. This would involve making an alternative conduit of blood to his leg via a bypass graft that I would create using a plastic type of pipe. I went on to explain to the wife that if God's native anatomy can fail, then it is understandable that anything that I could offer in terms of man-made material had a lesser chance of long-term success.

Her answer was, "Yes, I understand, but you can't sue God!"

This kind of mentality negatively affects the bond between doctor and patient. Physicians enjoy a tremendous privilege in the honor of handling the human body. Our decisions have far-reaching impacts on patients' lives. It is an honor and a tremendous privilege to have patients willingly allow me to take a sharp knife, open their bodies up, and handle their internal organs in any way I please. This is not something I take lightly. I invest a lot of time, energy, and emotional and mental commitment to my patients' well-being. When things don't go well for my patients, I take it personally. It affects my entire life. I have sleepless nights spent worrying about my patients' well-being. My family notices the effect it has on me. This kind of relationship should not be reduced to a legal contract between doctor and patient as is sometimes done when patients exhibit the attitude I described above.

There is no question that there is bad medicine being practiced. Sometimes this is a result of simple human error and sometimes a result of poor-quality physicians. Not all physicians are created equal. Some are better than others. It's a fact! We have a system of checks and balances that ensure the public safety by enforcing certification standards. As a surgeon, I have to finish medical school and then go through a residency program where I function under the supervision of senior surgeons and gain progressively more responsibility for the care of my patients. When I have successfully completed my residency and demonstrated the required knowledge and skill, then I am allowed to sit for a written board-certification exam that is administered by the American Board of Surgery. Following that, after a stint of further training (subspecialization) or a period of practice, I sit for another exam, an oral one this time, where I am evaluated by several senior surgeons. Once I pass that, I get to say that I am board certified by the American Board of Surgery. Having done that, I can prove to the public that I have what it takes to do the job. Doctors must also recertify every ten years to prove their competency. Annual state medical license renewal requirements also mandate a certain number of continuing medical education hours.

All board-certified surgeons go through the same process. If they chose further training (cardio-thoracic, vascular, etc.), there are specialty boards for those disciplines as well. Obtaining a medical license from the state and getting credentialed and privileged to perform surgery at a hospital requires a lengthy and exhaustive process of verification of training and certification.

So as you can see, there is a rigorous process in place to make sure that the public is safe. Now that doesn't mean that all surgeons are going to be the same. There are going to be human differences; some of us will be more skilled in certain functions than others. Some will take five hours to do what others might do in two. Some are going to fail their certification exams and have to take them over. If doctors repetitively fail, they have to go back for further training before they can retake the exams. Some are going to be skilled academicians who might be excellent at research and teaching but not so skilled in the operating room. Similarly, others might be great technicians but not so good at diagnosing or managing a complex disease process. Some will have better bedside manner than others. A few fortunate ones will have all the skill sets to set them apart from the rest.

Part of the system of checks and balances involves trending a surgeon's performance. Peer review involves colleagues evaluating bad outcomes, whether morbidity (complications) or mortality (death), and discussing the matter. If a surgeon has an excessively high complication rate, he or she may be counseled, suspended, expelled from the medical staff, or have limitations placed on his or her practice, such as getting more training, having another surgeon work with him or her for a period of time, etc.

Despite all of the requirements placed on doctors, bad medicine will continue to be practiced, and there will always be bad doctors practicing it. It is the responsibility of the state to protect its citizens from bad medicine. When a patient suffers a bad outcome because of negligence on the part of the doctor, something needs to be done. If the bad outcome is a result of a potential complication that was known to the patient and was not due to any fault of the physician, and if that physician is in good standing with normal performance statistics, then it is not negligence. But if that physician has repetitively had bad outcomes, did not meet the standard of care, or was not qualified to do what was done, then negligence might be at hand.

Two things need to happen. First, we must prevent this particular physician from hurting other people, and second, the patient who suffered the bad outcome should be compensated. In our current system, the first premise is not done. When a physician loses a lawsuit, the malpractice insurance company pays, his or her rates might go up, and unless there was a performance standards violation identified by peer review, then he or she goes on about business as usual.

Something is wrong with this picture. If a doc is found guilty of negligence, said doc should have some kind of restriction applied to his or her practice of medicine. If the doc failed to diagnose the disease correctly or performed the wrong operation or the right operation incorrectly, further training or supervision should be required before he is allowed to do the same thing again on his own.

In our current system, the wronged patient gets compensated, either as a settlement or by trial. Tort trials are exceedingly expensive, so insurance companies have a financial incentive to settle out of court to reduce their out-of-pocket cost. This does not involve an admission of guilt. It is simply a business decision. Lawyers capitalize on this by harassing defendants and intimidating them into settlement, frequently asking for the insured's policy limits. Each hospital has different requirements regarding the caps on malpractice insurance coverage. Some will require $100,000/$300,000 limits per event/aggregate, others $1,000,000/$3,000,000, depending on their malpractice environment. The plaintiff's attorney can make a good chunk of change by demanding policy limits, and it might be cheaper for the insurance company to settle than to go to trial. That's how it works. The ones who do go to trial and win can get exorbitant compensations.

The questions to ask are: *Who should determine if malpractice was committed? How should victims be compensated? How should plaintiff attorneys be compensated?*

Currently anyone can sue for any perceived wrong, and any lawyer can take on the case if he or she thinks there is merit to settle or take the case to court. This should not be so. A fair solution is to have medical certifying and licensing bodies review the case before allowing a lawsuit to be filed. Currently, when a patient contacts the

Texas Medical Board with a grievance about the conduct of a physician, the board investigates by requesting the medical records and renders an opinion. The investigating body consists of doctors, lawyers, and representatives from the public at large. If no wrongdoing was found, the case is dismissed. The patient is informed that no wrongdoing was identified, and the case is closed. If, on the other hand, there is a question on appropriateness of care, the physician will appear before the board (at his own expense) to defend himself, in which case he may win his argument or be found guilty of wrongdoing and face further penalties. A formal lawsuit can be filed at any time regardless of whether the medical board finds wrongdoing or not. Review by the medical board is not a prerequisite for filing a lawsuit.

If I get a patient with acute appendicitis and treat him, and he has a bad outcome, then this case should be reviewed by the licensing body—the Texas Medical Board—and in addition by the board certification body—the American Board of Surgery. These are the august bodies that have certified me as a specialist in the field of surgery and given me the license to practice my craft in this great state. Who would know better if I had done wrong? As I mentioned earlier, the Texas Medical Board committee consists of doctors, lawyers, and members of the public. The Texas Medical Board and the American Board of Surgery have no vested interest in the outcome of the case. They are not being compensated if the case is favorable or unfavorable. They form objective parties without prejudice. They truly are experts in the field, unlike the prosecutor's expert witness, who is frequently a hired gun and has a tremendous personal stake in the outcome because he is being compensated to support the prosecution. If wrongdoing is found, then the case could be litigated.

If a lawsuit is filed, the physician should be able to have his case defended by utilizing all information available, presented in a clear and understandable way. The medical field is very complicated. It is very difficult for the lay public to comprehend the intricacies of the practice of medicine. It is our duty to make it easy for them to understand what's going on. The current system does not allow that. There are so many restrictions on admissibility of data due to varied and sundry legal regulations. Expert witnesses are harassed and muzzled. They are not permitted to tell their stories in a clear or comprehensive way. They cannot elaborate or explain. They can only answer the question that was asked. It's not that easy. Certain medical questions don't have a yes or no answer. Complex decisions need complex explanations that need to be simplified for the jury. Plaintiff attorneys make that difficult to do. The jury should be exposed to an uncensored explanation of the facts by both the plaintiff and the defense, as if they were sitting in their living room hearing both sides of the argument. We need to simplify the process. If the jury finds the guy guilty after that process, then penalize him, but make it a fair process, for the love of God!

The next question is how the victim should be compensated. It is reasonable to assign a monetary value to the economic impact the wrongdoing caused the patient to suffer. Similarly, the pain and suffering incurred should be compensated. All this needs to be done in a reasonable fashion. Consider an eighty-two-year-old nursing home patient who falls and fractures his hip, goes on to develop pneumonia brought about by being immobilized from the sustained hip fracture, and dies. This case is quite different from a fifty-two-year-old diabetic working man who gets the wrong leg amputated for toe gangrene.

There should be limits on noneconomic damages. When they are unlimited, these astronomical awards serve no function other than to pad lawyers' pockets and drive up the cost of health care. The eighty-two-year-old nursing home patient shouldn't have fallen. But would it make a difference for you to know that he was also demented, abusive, and uncooperative, thus needing restraints? Would it make a difference for you to know that his family didn't like the use of restraints? Would it make a difference for you to know that he was on dialysis, had been in a nursing home for three years with no quality of life whatsoever, and that his family came to visit him only once a month? How about the fact that he had outlived his expected life span? Are you following my train of thought here? Yes, he suffered as a result of the fall, which should not have occurred, but how bad was that suffering? What amount of responsibility did he and his family have regarding the fall? How much economic loss resulted as a consequence? How much loss of companionship was there if the patient was demented and visited by his family once a month?

The nursing home should be investigated regarding their restraint and fall avoidance practices, and recommendations should be made and implemented to decrease the risk of this happening again. But we are not going to eliminate each and every risk of a complication from ever happening.

I have shown you that states that implement caps on noneconomic (punitive) damages have less malpractice and better physician retention rates (see the AMA citations in the bibliography). Let's be fair—fair to our citizens and fair to our doctors. We are alienating young people from entering medical school as the medical malpractice environment, Medicare and Medicaid payment cutbacks, and the increasing cost of medical education and practice take their tolls on the practice of medicine. The AAMC (American Association of Medical Schools) predicts an ongoing shortage of medical school applicants compared to the projected population growth. According to the American Medical Association, approximately 25 percent of our doctors are international medical graduates because our medical schools do not graduate enough doctors to fill all the residency training slots.[19]

The final question is how should malpractice plaintiff attorneys be compensated? I have given you sound arguments in chapter 3 as to why their logic for contingency fees is flawed. No other legal branch other than personal injury, medical malpractice, and workers' compensation cases are billed on a contingency basis. If we eliminate this huge incentive, I can assure you the number of malpractice suits will drop. Hardworking lawyers should be rewarded for the work that they do, just like hardworking doctors, businessmen, teachers, and so on. Success-based incentivization can be argued till the cows come home. Some are for it and some against. I have shown you the impact this practice has on the cost of health care. If we take middle-of-the-road stand and allow some form of contingency, then let's set limits—reasonable limits like England did. Put a cap on the increased earnings over and above the customary fee that can be garnished if the outcome is successful.

The Business of Medical Billing

Medical billing is a very complex business. Traditionally, procedure-oriented specialties (surgery) are compensated more than primary-care specialties. This is understandable because there is usually more training involved and more risk taking on behalf of the practitioner. In an effort to lessen this difference, the RVU (relative value unit) was developed. This is a yardstick that measures the amount of time and cognitive effort a nonprocedure-oriented physician puts into patient encounters. This allows for progressively higher compensation based on the complexity of the case at hand. It makes sense—the more difficult

---

19   www.ama-assn.org/ama/pub/category/211.html.

the case, the more you get paid. This system has generated different billing and documentation codes that doctors use to submit their bill.

A typical history and physical examination (H&P) consists of the following:

Chief complaint: Why the patient is here, in his own words.

History of present illness: A detailed interrogation documenting the main problem that caused the patient to seek attention. How and when did the complaint start, how has it progressed, what are the associated factors, exacerbating and relieving factors, and so on. The doctor is a detective at work trying to tease out valuable information from the patient and any others who can fill in the details of the story.

Medical history: A cataloguing of the patient's other medical diagnoses.

Surgical history:

Medications:

Allergies:

Family history:

Social history: Tobacco and alcohol consumption, use of illicit drugs, marital and sexual status.

Review of Systems: A detailed questionnaire of symptoms that might be present in each and every body system to help tease out undiagnosed diseases. For example, you are going for a hernia surgery, and I ask you about your bleeding tendencies. You say yes, you bleed forever when you cut yourself shaving. Bingo, I just found a problem I need to fix before I operate.

After the history is taken, a detailed physical exam follows.

General appearance:

Health-Care Reform: A Surgeon's Perspective

Vital signs:
Head and neck:
Chest, lungs and heart:
Abdomen, including rectal and genital exam:
Extremities:
Back:
Neurological:
Mental status:
Skin:

Each one of these entries in the H&P may be a standard abbreviation, a complex documentation, or a simple statement such as "unremarkable." The more thorough and comprehensive the documentation, the higher the bill that can be generated.

If I see a patient in consultation in my office I may use a level one to a level five consult depending on the complexity of the case, the amount of documentation generated, the treatment plan generated, and so on. If I see the patient back in follow-up, I can charge for an established patient visit between a level one and a level three. If the patient is seen in the hospital, the code is a hospital visit for a new nonconsult—a new patient admitted by me but not in consultation from another physician—or established patient level one through three, and one through five if seen in consultation again depending on the complexity of the encounter.

Okay, what if I see the patient today and operate on him tomorrow? I don't get to bill for the consultation because it's considered part of the global fee and built into the compensation schedule. But wait a moment, if I see him today and operate next week, I can bill for the consult. Wow, that makes a lot of sense! But there is something I can do to get paid for doing surgery the same day as I see him. I can use a modifier fifty-seven, which tells the government I made a decision to operate, so I can and should get paid for the consult. Then once I operate, I can't charge for my follow-up care for ninety days because it is considered part of the global fee, and that is built into the compensation schedule.

Now how do I determine which level of consult to charge? Well, that is based on the extent of documentation I put into the medical record and the complexity of the encounter. If I see a twenty-two-year-old man for a hangnail, I don't charge as much as if I am seeing a seventy-four-year-old diabetic smoker with heart disease who is going to have an aneurysm operation. That is fair. So what can I do to capture all the charges I can? Why, buff up the chart, of course. I fill in as much information as I can so I can charge more. My electronic medical record can come to the rescue. Through the use of templates and macros, I can generate sheaves of meaningless information to pad my bill. The more I document, the more I bill. The question is, who determines whether it is a level one or a level five consult? I do. But what if I am wrong? Why I get fined for Medicare fraud, of course. If you ask five different Medicare consultants (and I have), you will get five different answers as to what constitutes a level one or a level five and which level your particular encounter falls under. The safe thing to do is to under bill and stay below Medicare's radar, right? Wrong. If you consistently under bill, you fall out of the normal bell curve distribution on charges, and that alerts their radar. You are damned if you do and damned if you don't.

A patient in the hospital who is admitted by his primary care provider with a full history and physical examination documented on the chart is seen by a consultant, let's say a gastroenterologist. He dictates another comprehensive consult restating all of the information present in the initial H&P, thus billing for a higher level of care. Then said patient gets a surgical consult, and it's the same thing over again. The chart is padded with meaningless ramblings ad nauseam to allow for the highest billable charges. Frequently this information is copied from the initial H&P. Frequently it is not pertinent to the case at hand and contributes nothing to managing the patient.

For example, let's say I get called in to evaluate a patient with a high fever, abdominal pain, and a high white blood count. The primary doctor thinks it's a gall bladder problem. Now, I can do a full comprehensive H&P consultation and bill for it, or I can put a paragraph on the chart stating my pertinent findings and why I don't think it is a gall bladder problem, what I think it is, and what my recommendations are. I write a paragraph versus a several-page document. The bottom line is the pertinent information is going to be present in both. But I get paid more if I pad it up.

The medical billing process used to be quite simple. With a new patient encounter, there was a fixed price. For a follow-up visit, there was a fixed price. Charges were submitted to the patient, who paid up front, or to the insurance company. The office was staffed by a medical assistant and a business person who was the receptionist, biller, and coder all in one.

Health-Care Reform: A Surgeon's Perspective

Not so anymore. A typical practice has a receptionist, a biller, a coder (sometimes combined), a medical assistant or two, and an office manager to manage all the human resource issues and run the practice. Bills are submitted electronically or by paper after filling in a complex set of documents to categorize the nature of the claim, and God help you if you are wrong. Then there are frequent denials, then appeals, and then denials then the appeals. More and more things are not being covered by the insurance industry.

Let me give you an example of a recent encounter I had with Medicare. I had a patient with large, painful, and disfiguring lipomas (benign fatty tumors) that were growing in both his arms. He wanted them out. It should have been pretty straightforward. I scheduled him for surgery, but my biller informed me that Medicare wouldn't pay for this service because it is considered to be cosmetic. Well, I'm sorry, I disagree. This was not a simple, single growth but a complex number of large tumors that were stretching the patient's skin and compressing surrounding structures. Even if it were considered cosmetic, didn't this patient deserve to feel good about his body and not be embarrassed to go out in public with exposed arms?

I informed my biller that I would make arrangements to have the patient pay his bill personally, and to decrease his fee, I would do the procedure in my office under local anesthesia because the majority of the expense incurred comes from the hospital bill, not my bill. *Nope*, can't do that, Doc. We are Medicare providers (we accept discounted Medicare payments, so Medicare pays us directly rather than giving the money to the patient), so by law, I am not allowed to bill the patient directly. So what do I do here? Doc, you can only bill Medicare and wait for their denial after you have performed the procedure. Then we can appeal the denial, at which time it will be denied again. Only after a predetermined number of denials will I be allowed to bill the patient, who will have long had the procedure and would not be under any pressure to pay me. What kind of nonsense is this?

The increasing quagmire of government red tape, complex coding and billing regulations, and the increased administrative costs of staffing all the people that complicate the process is stifling and choking the system. We need to shed the layers of complexity and simplify the process. Let's go back to the simplicity of fixed pricing. It all evens out in the long run. Tough appendix today, easy one tomorrow; I get paid the same. I sweat it out today and sail through it tomorrow. Each encounter should be a fixed price, whether you document fifteen pages or two paragraphs. An in-hospital GI consult should have a fixed dollar amount; a cardiac consult should have same thing. This has already been implemented with regard to hospital compensation through the DRG (diagnosis-related group) policy. When a patient gets admitted with community-acquired pneumonia, the hospital gets paid a certain amount regardless of how much it spends on patient care.

Social Compromise and Sacrifice

As a society, we have to make some tough choices. We make these all the time in surgical triage—the massive bus accident, the tornado catastrophe, the mass casualties from a terrorist attack. As surgeons, we have to decide who is worth saving, who has the highest likelihood of being saved, and how we can better serve everyone by conserving our resources. It's not nice, kind, or humane, but it is practical, and it has to be done. This is something we teach our junior doctors in decision-making algorithms.

Do I tie up precious resources saving the eighty-nine-year-old grandma with life-threatening injuries, or do I focus on the fifteen-year-old girl with survivable injuries if I can address them quickly? It's like playing God, but *it has to be done!* Life is rough, and it is not fair. We cannot live forever, and we have to make tough choices.

The same can be said about our medical resources as a social community. We have lots of obligations. We have to provide a general health-care umbrella of vaccination and general social medical care. We have to take care of emergent medical and surgical conditions, such as heart attacks and trauma. We have to provide for our senior citizens with nursing home care.

As a society, we have to do all these things. The tough part comes when we have to decide how to allocate our resources. You have no idea how many elderly patients with no quality of life are on life-support measures such as ventilators and dialysis machines for extended periods of time. These are demented nursing home patients who do not recognize themselves or their family members. They are debilitated, with multiple bed sores and contractures and multiple medical problems. We keep flogging them with repeated hospital admissions, antibiotics, invasive procedures, and hundreds of thousands of dollars of tests and interventions.

Health-Care Reform: A Surgeon's Perspective

As I mentioned in chapter 2, "Comparative Health Care Delivery Models across the World," other countries have a much more realistic outlook on life. Terminally ill patients are not kept alive at whatever cost. Euthanasia is an accepted practice. Normal, everyday ills and suffering are accepted as part of everyday life and not subjected to numerous, expensive evaluations and treatments.

We have to be realistic with regard to our expectations. We cannot keep our loved ones alive forever at any cost. Life is a terminal illness and eventually comes to an end. We need to let that happen with humanity and dignity. We need to conserve our resources and ration them out according to the "greatest good for the greatest amount of people" concept of utilitarian ethics.

Do we allocate more of our health-care dollars toward our young in preventive health-care initiatives, or should we spend more on our elderly who have limited life expectancies? It is a tough question but one that has to be answered. There isn't enough to go round for everyone. It's a fact!

My father spent the last years of his life in a Canadian nursing home. He had been in a deteriorating state of health for several years. He had supportive care to keep him comfortable. When he fell and hit his head, developing an intracranial hemorrhage (head bleed) at age ninety, the Canadian system provided comfort measures. It was not good for society to spend valuable health-care dollars on terminally ill patients who had already outlived their life expectancies. The nursing home physician stated that my dad had suffered a head bleed and that given his age and overall condition, nothing further was going to be done. My dad was allowed to pass with dignity and peace. In the United States, he would have been subjected to a trip to the ER, a CT scan of the head, a neurosurgery consultation, a trip to the OR, a craniotomy, and a long and protracted death in a neurosurgical ICU. This would have cost the average citizen hundreds of thousands of dollars.

He was my dad. I loved him! I didn't want to lose him, but all considered, it was his time to go. He had no meaningful quality of life. He was debilitated by Parkinson's disease. He couldn't swallow his food. He was miserable. He was ninety years old and had outlived the average life expectancy of the usual adult North American male. It was his time, and I let him go!

We all have to make these decisions. But unfortunately, so many members of our society keep hanging on to unrealistic expectations and flogging their loved ones to unrealistic levels of suffering by holding on to lost hopes and dreams. They do this with no thought of financial consequences or social, personal, or societal impact. The indigent have no financial responsibilities and therefore have no financially vested interest in the impact of their decisions. They do not have to pay for any of the provided care, and neither do they understand the societal implications of the cost of care that they have chosen. They do not participate in preventative care, healthy lifestyles, or timely intervention for health-care issues. However, they expect our society to pay for extended unrealistic care for terminally ill family members regardless of the cost to our society as a whole. And God help you if you were to screw up, because you're going to get sued up the wazoo!

Socioeconomic status (SES) corresponds with health status without a doubt. According to the Centers for Disease Control, socioeconomic status as a multifactorial measure of educational attainment, household income, employment, wealth, access to goods and services, and the knowledge that these resources afford those who have them is a great determinant of morbidity and mortality as well as health dollar expenditures. Those of lower SES are less likely to be insured; less likely to seek preventative health care; less likely to receive appropriate vaccinations and health-screening measures (mammography, colonoscopy); less likely to receive prenatal care; more likely to make lifestyle choices that are detrimental to their health (tobacco use, practicing unprotected sex); and more likely to die younger. This is exemplified by the fact that between 2000 and 2010, emergency department usage by children and adults under the age of sixty-five years of age was highest among those with Medicaid coverage.[20]

We have to come to terms with the financial facts of health care, and we must dissociate our decisions from the influences of our malpractice attorneys. We should be able to make meaningful decisions based on the merits of the arguments at hand. We should have realistic expectations that are not artificially inflated by attorneys who promise a financial reward for perceived pain and suffering and wrongful death at no cost to the grieving families.

If we do not learn how to allocate our resources, someone else will do it for us. That's not usually pretty. We will abdicate our autonomy to some higher power that will mandate how we do business. If we are

---

20   http://www.cdc.gov/nchs/data/hus/hus11.pdf#133.

to avoid this, we must be realistic and do the socially responsible thing that will satisfy the masses under the provisions of utilitarian ethics.

Our lifestyle is destroying our health. Our schools need to offer healthier lunch and snack menus, incorporate more physical exercise in the education curriculum, and work closely with families to ensure that nutritional goals are in harmony between school and home. When I was a kid, there were a few TV channels and no Internet, computers, e-mail, MySpace, or Facebook. I spent my free time riding my bike, climbing trees, chasing girls, and hanging out in the park. My grandfather went to work on a horse. My kids had Nintendo, Xbox, and all sorts of electronic entertainment outlets. We are spending less and less energy in our daily lives and consuming more and more calories. The majority of our jobs are sedentary desk jobs, relying on computers, phone lines, and text messages. Our parents frequently work two jobs to make ends meet, so there isn't enough time to prepare a healthy dinner. Fast food is a culinary staple in our modern society.

Our infrastructure is not designed to allow for physical exertion in activities of daily life. Most European cities can be negotiated on foot or by bicycle. Citizens frequently bike or walk to a commuter terminal, take mass transit, walk to work, climb stairs, and repeat the process on the way back. Going shopping is frequently done on bike or on foot. Not so in the United States. Some of our larger cities provide these options, but a lot of our towns, villages, and cities don't. I live in South Texas in a city with no public transportation, no usable sidewalks, and no urban planning. Urban design did not include proximity of shopping venues. I can't get out of my house and safely take a bicycle ride to a nearby market to buy groceries for dinner. I *have* to take my car, and that's just the way it was designed. Thereby, I have lost the opportunity to expend energy during my daily activities.

The abundance of energy, real estate, and urban sprawl in our earlier development led to shortsighted planning. I look around my city and see a trailer park followed by a restaurant, then an apartment complex, then a used tire store, then a nice home, then a used car mart, then another decent home followed by a fast-food restaurant. And all of this is on a stretch of a business highway. Our planners were wearing really dark sunglasses when they thought this nonsense up. The concepts of zoning and communal development completely evaded them.

Social Entitlement Programs

We must modify the status quo. I'm all for social assistance and safety nets, but there has to be a cutoff. Our system is being raped by some of our citizens. Several of my patients are unemployed, obese, with several children, disabled, collecting unemployment or disability benefits, and receiving food stamps. The majority of these patients should not have been categorized as disabled. They cite numerous vague and sundry complaints, such as back pain, knee pain, and workman's compensation–related injuries, but after numerous MRIs, neurology, orthopedic, and neurosurgery consults, no definitive intervention was offered, so they continue to live off their fellow citizens because some misguided authority labeled them as disabled.

Got back pain? *Deal* with it. Get a goddamned job. I've got back pain from years of bending over an operating table. I broke my neck while doing an amputation, straining to divide a bone with shears. I had to have surgery to remove a piece of intervertebral disc that was impinging on my spinal cord. The joints of my hands are gnarled from years of overwork, with serious pain during and after extended surgeries. I have been told by hand surgeons that I need to have some joints fused, which would take me several months to recover from and possibly end my career. I know pain, but I will work, for crying out loud. And mind you, I have disability insurance! Got back pain? Get a job that doesn't strain your back.

Recently on the news, there was a feature about a nurse who was facing foreclosure on her home. She was "disabled" because she got a shoulder injury while applying pressure on the groin of a patient after a heart catheterization to stop the artery from bleeding! *Sorry!* Can't happen. We frequently use heavy sand bags to do the same thing. She could have done that. Applying downward pressure from a standing position with elbows locked does not strain the shoulder joint, especially if the applier of pressure is over two hundred pounds, which she was. Anyhow, somehow she was "disabled." *Why!* Isn't there any other nursing job in the country she could do without having to strain her shoulder? How about reviewing patients' charts, handing out medicines, becoming a school nurse, or something! Why should she live off the rest of society without contributing another day's work?

Sadly, that is the same way I feel about the majority of "disabled" patients who cross my path. Some people truly are in need of disability protection, but they are the few and far between.

Health-Care Reform: A Surgeon's Perspective

How about the obese, twenty-five-year-old mother of four who hasn't worked a day in the last ten years? She comes in for a gall bladder surgery consult. She is covered in hickeys and gold chains. She sports a fancy purse and fake, manicured nails. Her equally obese, unemployed boyfriend is by her side glaring at me while I evaluate her. What's wrong with this picture? Why is she being supported for having more children through such programs as CHIP (Children's Health Insurance Program), WIC, and food stamps that exponentially offer more for each child that she has? I'm sorry, but if you are poor, unemployed, and starving, you should be working your ass off to find a job that will put an end to your misery. Rather than finding a job, she lives off society, which continues to support her. In most countries, poor people with lots of kids are working their butts off. They are usually thin and don't sport fancy purses or manicured nails.

Yes, this patient needs help. Yes, as a society we have to take care of our citizens. But where does it end? Where does individual responsibility come into play? Should there not be a limit on how many children this unemployed person should have that everyone else is supporting? Should we not have some kind of work program where this citizen can contribute while her kids are cared for in a subsidized daycare center? I'm not preaching eugenics here. I'm just saying that we need to have a more reasonable support structure than what we have now. The system encourages unemployment, multiple children, and a lazy lifestyle by rewarding them with multiple benefits. As I have shown you before, it is easier to get assistance if you are unemployed than if you are employed in a low-income job that puts you above the cutoff line for assistance. There should be consequences to our actions.

Excluding senior-citizen Medicare recipients from my practice, somewhere between 30 to 50 percent of my patients do not contribute to our society's economic growth. They are takers, not givers. They do not hold regular jobs. They are obese or morbidly obese. They are well dressed and sport fine accoutrements, and they have lots and lots of kids. As a matter of fact, they are having more kids than their better-off counterparts who do have jobs and contribute to our economic growth.

I don't have an answer to this problem, but I do know it is a problem that needs to be addressed. There are numerous scenarios as to how we can go about solving this problem, and like anything else, there will be controversy among individuals. What we need to realize is that we cannot continue along this path of business as usual. This is a recipe for disaster. We are raping our health-care resources, and we don't have any meaningful solutions to the problems that plague our system. We cannot hide our heads in the sand and carry on as usual. An ounce of prevention is worth more than a pound of cure. We need to radically modify the status quo to prevent our impending future collapse.

Universal Coverage

You know my position on this subject. I have made it abundantly clear that all our citizens should have health insurance. How we should do this is a subject of debate. I don't know that there is one best solution, but something better surely exists. As I have demonstrated, there are different models we can emulate.

The available models to choose from are the single-payer, two-tier, or insurance-mandate models, which I have described previously. I am strongly opposed to a single-payer system in which the government either provides nationalized health care or insures it through nationalized insurance where health care is administered through governmental agencies. The military is about the only thing I trust the government with, which they can do well. Any other government enterprise is fraught with red tape and inefficiency.

Look at the Veterans' Administration hospital, and compare it to any other hospital nearby (there usually is one, thank God). I have worked at VA hospitals and numerous for-profit and not-for-profit hospitals. The VA is a paragon of inefficiency. *Never has so little been done by so many for so much!* I'm not kidding. For the size of the facility, the number of employees, and the allocated budget, there is less work generated at a greater cost. There is a mountain of red tape that has to be negotiated to get anything done. Given the same resources at a private hospital, you can accomplish double the productivity at a fraction of the cost.

The VA tends to attract employees of a lesser caliber than comparable hospitals in similar locations—usually elder physicians who are looking forward to slowing down or foreign doctors. Sorry, I am not out to offend anyone; I am just noting fact here. According to the American Medical Association, international medical graduates make up about a quarter of our physician work force in this country (25.3 percent), and just over a quarter of physicians in training or residents (27.8 percent).[21] It is a

---

21   http://www.ama-assn.org/ama1/pub/upload/mm/18/img-workforce-paper.pdf.

matter of supply and demand. There are more positions available to be filled than our medical schools can supply. Foreign-trained medical doctors fill this void.

Once foreign physicians have completed their training, they have to leave the country, unless they can manage to find a way to stay in the United States. One of the most common ways to stay is to find a job that allows for an exemption from the US immigration and naturalization policy, which is to serve in an underserved area. Yup, you got it—the VA is considered one of those safe havens. Because the VA has difficulty filling available positions with American medical doctors, it resorts to hiring international medical graduates. According to Christopher Lee of the *Washington Post*, VA Secretary Anthony Principi stated that there is a critical shortage of physicians in the VA system. This is thought to be due to a more than 35 percent lag in VA salaries compared to the private sector.[22]

The security of a government paycheck, the generous benefits, and the lack of pressure to produce attracts a certain kind of individual. In addition, the malpractice environment at the VA is quite different from the private practice environment. In the VA, physicians are salaried. Job benefits include paid malpractice insurance among the other usual government benefits. If there is a case that raises a malpractice concern, it is referred to a board within the VA that decides the outcome. VA employees are generally immune from being sued individually, placing their employer as the suit target as long as the employees were acting under their job descriptions. The VA, however, can be sued under the Federal Court Claims Act.[23] Rarely do VA physicians have to appear in front of a jury in a tort case to defend themselves. Their malpractice premiums are not subject to change because of frequency of suits or the riskiness of their particular practice compared to a private practice physician.

In general, these factors lead to hiring a certain kind of individual. That individual is less likely to be competitive, more likely to be lazy and less driven, and more likely to be an international medical graduate. I'm sorry, but these are just the facts. I am a physician of foreign origin, so I have more of a license to criticize my own kind. I'm not saying that all foreign doctors are bad; not at all. The majority of them are excellent

---

22   http://www.washingtonpost.com/wp-dyn/articles/A62681-2004Jul19.html.

23   http://www.veteranstoday.com/2010/09/17/finding-complaints-malpractice-claims-disciplinary-action-against-va-health-care-practitioners/.

physicians. There are, however, language and cultural barriers that exist, making them less competitive in the workplace. American-trained physicians are less likely to accept the lower salaries and bureaucratically stifling work environment than their foreign counterparts. The organizational culture of the VA then takes over and promotes a lack of productivity.

This is not an isolated sentiment but a view that is held by the majority of my colleagues. There is an established saying in the halls of academia that the best thing about a VA hospital is that there is a real hospital nearby, referring to a university teaching hospital. They usually are in close proximity to most major VA hospitals.

The majority of my hospital practice is at a large not-for-profit private community hospital with a university academic affiliation. I can do ten to twelve cases a day at this hospital. On my surgery block days, I can post as many cases as I can do in a day. I frequently get two or three rooms and flip-flop my cases so I don't have to wait for one room to be turned over. This allows me to get two or three teams (nurses, OR techs, anesthesia personnel). I can do this and teach medical students and residents at the same time. On some days I will have five to six cases, others ten to twelve, depending on the complexity of the cases involved. I will frequently be done by the late afternoon.

If you even think or dream of doing this at a VA or state university hospital, you will be laughed out of town. The bottleneck occurs by early afternoon, so you will be lucky to do one or two large cases and maybe three or four quick cases. You will not have two or three rooms to flip-flop. The entire team has no incentive to do more but to do less. They get paid the same regardless of how hard they work. The system is not designed to promote efficiency. There are neither productivity metrics nor consequences for falling below them. Dragging feet and procrastinating are the norm. Finding barriers and roadblocks to productivity are built into the system. The quagmire of government red tape stifles any kind of performance improvement initiative. The security of a "government" job from which you cannot get fired unless you are caught screwing a patient in the recovery room leads to a certain mind-set for the employees. There is no competition to deal with; there is a captive audience with no alternatives.

If I see a patient who is forty-two years old and who is healthy overall who needs a groin hernia repaired in my office, I could very likely schedule him for surgery next week as a day surgery procedure,

Health-Care Reform: A Surgeon's Perspective

where he comes in the morning of surgery and goes home the same day. But this is not so at the VA! Oh, a hernia. Well let's see now, you need a proctoscopy—an exam of the anus and rectum with a rigid scope—first to make sure you don't have a lower gastrointestinal reason for you to be constipated and hence straining at stool, thus getting a hernia. Never mind that you don't have any symptoms of constipation or a family history of colon-rectal cancer. You are scheduled to have a proctoscopy in three weeks.

Then you follow up with your doctor to schedule surgery. Day surgery—ha, ha, ha! Oh no, you must come in a day or two before your operation to get checked out. Let's do some blood work, an EKG, a chest X-ray, and whatever else we can muster up—stuff that is usually done as an outpatient if need be. But your surgery date got postponed because the budget ran short, so the VA is shutting down one or two operating rooms to offset the costs of doing business for a few weeks until they can figure out how to manage the budget. Then your surgery is scheduled in six weeks. Come on in to the VASPA. You'll have one or two days of before-surgery hospitality, then surgery, and then go home, right? Oh no you don't. You're not ready to go home yet. How about another week in the hospital because of certain social issues or because you don't feel quite right to go home just yet? Contrast this to a private practice experience where all straightforward hernia surgeries are done on an outpatient basis.

Do you get my point here? I can offer the same service at a fraction of the cost without the bureaucracy involved in the VA system. In addition, the system utilized by the VA offers no health-care advantages whatsoever. It offers no cost savings at all. In fact, it does quite the opposite. It escalates the cost of care. It follows the organizational culture promulgated by the government. The government security, lack of accountability, and lack of performance metrics analysis encourage doctors to take the easy way out every single time. The less I can do, the more hurdles I can throw at the problem. The less effort I expend and the less desire for efficiency and accountability, the better! That is the organizational culture at the VA. Ask doctors who don't work at the VA but who rotated there during their training, and they will share my same sentiment, unanimously!

No, I don't think a single-payer system is the answer. We need competition and free enterprise. That leaves us with an insurance mandate or a two-tier system. Both are okay. An insurance mandate basically is a requirement that is imposed by the government on health insurers to mandate provision of insurance to the citizens. A two-tier system allows for some form of governmental insurance over and above which citizens can buy additional coverage.

Both are not exclusive of each other, and some features can overlap. The ideal condition would be for all citizens to have coverage. This can be accomplished through government-mandated insurance with a base package funded by the government and contracted out to private insurers. Citizens are then free to add other features to their plans. By keeping the insurance providers in the private sector, we promote capitalist economic advantages. By paying for standard coverage through tax-based funding we assure insurance for everyone.

A seventy-year-old retired man with a groin hernia can afford to wait a month or two to get it taken care of. The fifty-two-year-old business owner, who wants it fixed yesterday so he can get on with his life, can afford to buy supplemental insurance. Both will get taken care of comparably, but one will enjoy better advantages for the extra money that he is dishing out. Catastrophic coverage will be available to all. Denial of coverage due to preexisting conditions will be outlawed!

A two-tier system will allow for universal base coverage for all, followed by employer contributions and finally employee contributions to the plan. Health systems will be contracted with based on performance metrics. How much will it cost for you take care of the insured patient overall? How well do you measure up to published benchmarks? Do you have a lot of overzealous interns ordering CAT scans right and left to diagnose hangnails, or are you thrifty with your dollar?

Again, I don't have all the final answers. A lot of work still needs to be done, but I am laying the ground work for a revamped health-care system. None of these changes are the cure-all for our problems. They all need to work together to achieve meaningful reform. I am tired of politicians with lofty goals who talk and talk and accomplish nothing. We need to act and act now. Our government is broke, and there is no solution or end in sight. Business as usual is not an option. We need radical reform, not fine-tuning of the system. This will involve serious change and sacrifice by many, but that's the way anything of value gets done. And while we are on the subject of our government, let's set some accountability standards.

To open up a barber shop, I have to have a license that is granted by an overseeing, governing body. To practice medicine, I encounter the same

Health-Care Reform: A Surgeon's Perspective

thing. I have to provide evidence of adequate training and demonstrate a thorough comprehension of the current practice guidelines. If I fall below the acceptable standard of care, there is hell to pay. I have to answer to governing bodies, licensing bodies, and certification bodies and face the threat of a lawsuit with serious financial implications. But what about our government? To become the president of the United States of America, all you need are two things: proof of birth in the country and being over the age of thirty-five. That's it! There are no certifying exams and no licensing or recertification required. You can wage war, make all sorts of decisions with far-reaching implications, and affect everyone's life, but you answer to no one! Unless you happen to screw a white house intern; then hell will let loose and you will face impeachment charges.

Our lawmakers, senators, and congressmen are not held to any accountability standards. They are not held to performance benchmarks. If the current administration states a policy and falls short of those stated accomplishments, nothing happens. If I fall short of accepted performance guidelines, I have hell to pay. I am posted on the Internet and compared to all the other practitioners in the field. My patients' grievances that have been filed against me are made publicly available. I can get sued for falling below the standard of care if I am not a good boy and practice substandard medicine.

Wait one freaking minute. What about our government? Is there no accountability for this august body? Are our lawmakers and our governors allowed to dig us into a hole that will put our grandchildren into lifelong debt? Is it okay for our government to fall way below our expected performance metrics? Should there be no consequences if we get royally screwed over by some governmental policy that proved to be a seriously bad idea? Should there be a certifying body that permits government officials to do their magic? Should this certifying body have authority to discipline folks who fall short of expected standards?

That seems like a double standard to me. But then again, let's not forget the golden rule: he who has the gold makes the rules! The lawyers who run our government make the rules. They are accountable to no one! The only thing that will get them thrown out of office or seriously reprimanded is a sex or ethics scandal, not a performance standard. The proverbial buck is tossed back and forth between our only two meaningful parties with such confusing statistics that you can never, ever know what the truth really is. Both parties speak to their accomplishments and to the deficiencies of the opposing party. They cite all sorts of "facts," which the opposing party will refute and then state some of their own "facts." In the end, it is a yo-yo of back-and-forth politicking, with lots of rhetoric and lofty goal announcements, always including the future of the children of *America*. And in the end, it's business as usual.

What we have is not a democracy but an oligarchy. Representation in government, for the people, by the people, and of the people is an altruistic goal. We have a good old boys' club of Yale, Harvard, and Princeton alumni who are in collusion with each other running the government. People like Dennis Hastert, the former speaker of the house with humble backgrounds as a high school wrestling coach, are rare in government. Our government has to be accountable and answer to our citizens. Health issues must be tackled and addressed by the government. Solutions to our problems must be presented for meaningful debate. Identified problems must have solutions proposed, implemented, tracked by performance metrics, and evaluated for effectiveness. Deterioration of health-care metrics must not be allowed. Just as health-care professionals and institutions are held to a certain standard that is transparently displayed to the public, government officials must be held to the same standard. They must be held accountable for public policy and performance of programs, with predetermined performance metrics held over their heads for comparison to stated goals.

Chapter 6: Postscript/Obamacare

Since I started writing this book, the Obamacare health-care policy reform has been widely debated and has gone up to the Supreme Court for a ruling on its constitutionality. With the Supreme Court divided along party lines, the tie-breaker ruling rendered by Chief Justice John Roberts has created an historic decision in favor of the health-care law. The whole world could see the Cheshire grin President Obama wore as he pronounced to the world the ruling of the Supreme Court in favor of his presidency defining health-care reform law.

Well, let's first address the issue of its constitutionality. Is it constitutional for the government to force its citizens to purchase health insurance? Well, what about Medicare? The government forces its citizens to pay a tax to cover the health-care needs of citizens over sixty-five. How then can it not be allowed to impose the same kind of tax to cover the health-care needs of its citizens who are under sixty-five? If the former is constitutional, then by inference, so is the latter! That is the opinion of Chief Justice John Roberts. He didn't reach this opinion without some fancy legal footwork to appease both sides of the aisle.

He first opined that congress lacked the power to force citizens to buy insurance that they didn't want to buy. Under the Commerce Clause, the government has regulatory powers over commerce but not on citizens who have not yet engaged in a commercial venture of purchasing health insurance. However, he went on to say that the health insurance mandate was actually a tax levied on citizens who chose to forego purchasing health insurance (tax, penalty, call it what you will), and thus it was within the powers of congress to levy taxes (Von Drehle, 2012).

As our country remains divided about this crucial issue, I am in favor of the health-care reform mandate. As you have read all along, I support some form of government-mandated health insurance policy. I have demonstrated from the beginning how I supported the United Nations Declaration of Human Rights Policy, which calls for citizens to have access to health care. I have demonstrated that most civilized countries have some form of mandatory health coverage. It is high time that we as a nation tackle this growing problem head-on with all its ramifications. This is a step in the right direction, but it must be followed by comprehensive reform, as I have outlined in this book. Mandating insurance without addressing all the drivers of escalating health-care costs will be a drop in the bucket toward comprehensive reform.

Like it or not, the Supreme Court has ruled Obamacare the law of the land. So what does that mean to you and me? After condensing down the twenty-four hundred pages of the Affordable Care Act, here are the nuts and bolts, which were recently summarized in a recent *Time* magazine issue (Von Drehle, 2012; Klein, 2012).

If you are a young adult under twenty-six, you can stay on your parent's policy. By 2014, if you are not covered under your parents' policy, you will have to purchase insurance if it is not provided by your employer or a government program. By not doing so, you will face a penalty. The catch is that it will probably cost you more since insurance companies will not be allowed to set premiums based on risk. They will not be allowed to factor in preexisting conditions, so the premiums will reflect a more even distribution rather than risk-based assessment of premiums.

If you are a low- to middle-income earner, in 2014 your income will determine your options. If you earn less than 133 percent of the federal poverty level ($14,856 in 2012), you may qualify for Medicaid. If you earn more than 133 percent of the poverty level but less than 400 percent ($44,680 in 2012) and don't have affordable insurance through your job, you may be eligible for government subsidies to help you purchase insurance independently.

If you are a small business owner employing twenty-five or fewer employees, you may be eligible for federal tax credits to help with the purchase of health insurance for your workers. If you employ fifty or

Health-Care Reform: A Surgeon's Perspective

more workers and you don't provide them with health insurance, or they can't afford the insurance that you have provided, you might be subjected to a fine. The good news is that depending on which state you for a less expensive option through a highly regulated insurance exchange.

If you are employed by a large company, there probably won't be much of a change for you. Your company will be required to provide you with a health insurance plan. You may opt out if you wish, but then you will be obliged to purchase a health insurance policy on your own. Federal regulations require that health insurance policies meet minimum standards, but you won't have a say in what kind of coverage or deductible you choose. It will be chosen for you.

If you are an elderly person enrolled in Medicare, preventative care such as annual checkups will be provided at no cost to you. You may receive deep discounts on generic drugs and a $250 rebate from the government to help offset the "doughnut hole"—the cost of prescription drugs that you individually bear between $2,930 and $4,700 coming directly out of your pocket. Over time, the doughnut hole should disappear; however, some benefits that you might have through a private insurance plan under the auspices of Medicare might disappear.

If you have a preexisting condition, you may be eligible for coverage by a high-risk insurance pool. Beginning in 2014, insurance companies will not be allowed to discriminate against people with preexisting conditions. They won't be able to turn you away or charge you a higher rate.

How does the government pay for this? If you earn more than $200,000 a year, your taxes will increase. If you are a company employing more than fifty workers and don't offer insurance, you will be fined. Nearly all Americans will have to have health insurance or face a fine, with some exceptions. If your total out-of-pocket expenses exceed 8 percent of your income after federal subsidies and employer contributions, you will be exempt from the federal penalty.

Interestingly, the fines levied upon individuals are to be collected by the Internal Revenue Service, with one caveat; if you refuse to pay, the Affordable Care Act will not allow the IRS to jail you or seize your property. So it's not so draconian after all!

To help even the playing field, the federal government has allowed individual states to opt in or out of expanding Medicaid, which is a federal and state-run program. The fed has also opened up the insurance market to interstate commerce, thus allowing out-of-state insurance companies to compete for clients in all states, thus allowing the free enterprise market forces to influence pricing.

For more information about the effect of Obamacare, I urge you to visit the Kaiser Family Foundation Health Reform Source at http://healthreform.kff.org. Also, a recent post on Reddit, the social media news site, does a great job of explaining Obamacare in plain language: http://www.reddit.com/r/explainlikeimfive/comments/vb8vs/eli5_what_exactly_is_obamacare_and_what_did_it/c530lfx.

Conclusion

I hope I have shed some light for you on how our health-care system works, how it compares to other systems across the world, what the cost drivers are, and how to fix the problem. This is not a comprehensive book but an introduction to the subject. As I said earlier, I don't pretend to have all the answers—just the general principles of what's wrong and how to fix it as viewed by a person who has been entrenched in the field for several decades, with a unique perspective based on the many hats that I wear.

We need a team with surgical or *Navy SEAL* characteristics to tackle this problem. This team will need to include doctors, lawyers, insurance industry representatives, lawmakers, and general public representatives. The problem will not be solved by mild-mannered bureaucrats. It needs a mind-set of extirpation of the current system, which is where the surgical, Navy SEAL mind-set comes in. We have to have an open mind and evaluate other systems without prejudice.

I approach this problem with a surgical mind-set. In surgery, we do not allow for mediocrity. We do not make half-assed decisions. We evaluate the problem at hand, develop potential solutions, and consider the best intervention, the pros and cons, the costs, the dangers, the sacrifices, and the potential outcomes, and then we make a decision. That decision is in the best interest of the patient and the family. These decisions are not easy. Sometimes they are gut-wrenching, and sometimes they have to be made in split seconds. But at the end of the day, we have to act, and our actions are available for all to see. Over the years, surgeons as a specialty have done very well. We have lived up to our goals as surgeons, promoted health care from the surgical perspective, and performed admirably as compared to benchmarked performance standards.

It is time for our government to be held to similar standards. We as a society must work together to accomplish our stated goals. This will involve serious dialogue between government, medical, business, insurance, and legal representatives, in addition to citizens at large.

I seriously hope that I have not offended anyone in this dialogue. It is impossible to address all these issues without painfully transparent discussions of all the issues at hand. One cannot hide behind political correctness and expect to accomplish anything. I have laid my heart out here on a subject that I feel passionately about and wish to influence in the course of my lifetime. I hope that I have opened your eyes and caught your attention. I hope that I have generated controversy to get people talking. I am optimistic that this dissertation will lead to public controversy, leading to more dialogue, with the end in sight of better public health policy. I will be glad to tackle these issues further with whomever wants to discuss them. I am sure that there is a better way out there, and I hope I can be part of the solution.

Bibliography

American Cancer Society. (2012). *American Cancer Society Guidelines for the Early Detection of Cancer.* Retrieved January 18, 2012, from American Cancer Society: http://www.cancer.org/Healthy/FindCancerEarly/CancerScreeningGuidelines/american-cancer-society-guidelines-for-the-early-detection-of-cancer.

American Medical Association. (2010). *Getting the most for our health care dollars: Medical liability reform.* Retrieved January 23, 2012, from   http://www.ama-assn.org/resources/doc/health-care-costs/medical-liability-reform.pdf.

American Medical Association. (n.d.). *The Case for Medical Liability Reform.* Retrieved January 23, 2012, from http://www.ama-assn.org/ama1/pub/upload/mm/-1/case-for-mlr.pdf.

Calfo, S. S. (2008). *Last Year of Life Study.* Retrieved December 30, 2011, from Centers for Medicare & Medicaid Services: https://www.cms.gov/ActuarialStudies/downloads/Last_Year_of_Life.pdf.

Committee on the Costs of Medical Care. (1932). *Medical Care for the American People.* Chicago: University of Chicago Press.

Commonwealth Fund. (2008). *Increase in Life Expectancy at Birth, 1986–2006.* Retrieved January 1, 2012, from Commonwealth Fund: http://www.commonwealthfund.org/Charts/Chartbook/Multinational-Comparisons-of-Health-Systems-Data-2008-FULL/Increase-in-Life-Expectancy-at-Birth.aspx.

Commonwealth Fund. (2009). *National Health Expenditures as a Percentage of Gross Domestic Product, 1960–2020.* Retrieved July 12, 2012, from Commonwealth Fund: http://www.commonwealthfund.org/Charts/Presidents-Column/Costs-of-Failure/NHE-as-a-Percentage-of-GDP-1960-2020.aspx.

Commonwealth Fund. (2009). *Potential Years of Life Lost Because of Diabetes, 2007.* Retrieved January 1, 2012, from Commonwealth Fund: http://www.commonwealthfund.org/Charts/Chartbook/Multinational-Comparisons-of-Health-Systems-Data-2009/Potential-Years-of-Life-Lost-Diabetes.aspx.

Commonwealth Fund. (2010). *Average Number of Physician Visits Per Capita, 2008.* Retrieved January 1, 2012, from Commonwealth Fund: http://www.commonwealthfund.org/Charts/Chartbook/Multinational-Comparisons-of-Health-Systems-Data-2010/A/Average-Annual-Number-of-Physician-Visits-per-Capita.aspx.

Commonwealth Fund. (2010). *Cost-Related Access Problems in the Past Year.* Retrieved January 1, 2011, from Commonwealth Fund: http://www.commonwealthfund.org/Charts/In-The-Literature/How-Health-Insurance-Design-Affects-Access/Cost-Related-Access-Problems.aspx.

Commonwealth Fund. (2010, June 23). *US Ranks Last Among Seven Countries on Health System Performance Based on Measures of Quality, Efficiency, Access, Equity, and Healthy Lives.* Retrieved December 30, 2011, from Commonwealth Fund: http://www.commonwealthfund.org/News/News-Releases/2010/Jun/US-Ranks-Last-Among-Seven-Countries.aspx.

Conway, Karen. (2011, August 10). Orlikoff on Healthcare: It's Killing America. Retreived July 12, 2012, from GXH Healthcare Hub Blog: http://www.ghx.com/product-pages/industry-resources/blog-thehealthcare-hub/entryid/27.aspx.

Dartmouth Atlas of Health Care. (2012). Retrieved January 18, 2012, from Dartmouth Atlas of Health Care: http://www.dartmouthatlas.org/.

Davis, Karen. (2012, January 18). Bending the Health Care Cost Curve: New Era in American Health Care? Retrieved July 10, 2012, from The Commonwealth Fund Blog: http://www.commonwealthfund.org/Blog/2012/Jan/Bending-the-Health-Care-Cost-Curve.aspx

Elshove-Bolk, J. (2004, October). A description of emergency department-related malpractice claims in The Netherlands: Closed claims study, 1993–2001. *European Journal of Emergency Medicine, 11*(5), 247–250.

Gawande, A. (2009, June 1). The Cost Conundrum. *New Yorker.*

Greider, K. (2003). *The Big Fix: How the Pharmaceutical Industry Rips Off American Consumers.* New York: Public Affairs.

Guardado, J. (2009). *Professional Liability Insurance Indemnity and Expenses, Claim Adjudication, and Policy Limits, 1999–2008.* American Medical Association.

Guerino, P. H. (2011, December). *Prisoners in 2010.* Retrieved January 18, 2012, from US Department of Justice: http://bjs.ojp.usdoj.gov/content/pub/pdf/p10.pdf.

Hogan, C. L. (2002). Medicare Beneficiaries' Cost of Care in the Last Year of Life. *Health Affairs, 20*(4), 189–195.

Institute of Medicine. (2001). *Crossing the Quality Chasm: A New Health System for the 21st Century.* Washington, DC: National Academy Press.

Kimia, A., et al. (2010). Yield of lumbar puncture among children who present with their first complex febrile seizure. *Pediatrics, 126*(1), 62–9.

Klazinga, N. (2008, February). *The Dutch Health Care System.* Retrieved December 30, 2011, from Commonwealth Fund: http://www.commonwealthfund.org/~/media/Files/Resources/2008/Health%20Care%20System%20Profiles/Netherlands_Country_Profile_2008%20.pdf.

Klein, J. (2012, June 29). And Now, How to Improve Obamacare. Retrieved August 15, 2012, from *Time Magazine*: http://swampland.time .com/2012/06/29/and-now-how-to-improve-obamacare/.

Lerner, B. (2011, August 14). A Life-Changing Case for Doctors in Training. *New York Times*.

Light, D. W., & Warburton, R. (2011). Demythologizing the high costs of pharmaceutical research. *Biosocieties*, 1–17.

Lubitz, J. D. (1993). Trends in Medicare Payments in the Last Year of Life. *New England Journal of Medicine, 328*(15), 1092–1096.

Maslow, A. (1943). A Theory of Human Motivation. *Psychological Review, 50*, 370–396.

National Breast Cancer Coalition. (2011, July). *Mammography for Breast Cancer Screening: Harm/Benefit Analysis*. Retrieved January 18, 2012, from National Breast Cancer Coalition: http://www.breastcancerdeadline2020.org/know/assets/documents/mammography-for-breast-cancer.pdf.

National Conference of State Legislatures. (2011, August). *Medical Liability/Medical Malpractice Laws*. Retrieved January 23, 2012, from http://www.ncsl.org/issues-research/banking-insurance-financial-services/medical-liability-medical-malpractice-laws.aspx.

Organisation for Economic Co-operation and Development. (2012). *OECD Health Data 2012: How Does the United States Compare?* Retrieved July 10, 2012, from Organisation for Economic Co-operation and Development: http://www.oecd.org/dataoecd/46/2/38980580.pdf.

Comparing International Health Care Systems (2009). [Motion Picture].

Plunkett, J. W. (2006). *Plunkett's Insurance Industry Almanac*. Houston, TX: Plunkett Research, Ltd.

Polder, J. (2006, October). Health care costs in the last year of life—the Dutch experience. *Social Science and Medicine, 63*(7), 1720–1731.

Rampell, C. (2010, August 13). Medical Care Prices Fell for First Time in 35 Years. *New York Times.*

Suddath, C. (2009, February 27). A Brief History of the Middle Class. Retrieved January 18, 2012, from *Time Magazine:* http://www.time.com/time/nation/article/0,8599,1882147,00.html.

Towers Watson (Perrin). (2006). *Towers Watson.* Retrieved January 18, 2012, from US Tort Costs and Cross Border Perspectives: 2005 Update: https://www.towersperrin.com/tillinghast/publications/reports/2005_Tort_Cost/2005_Tort.pdf.

Towers Watson. (2010). *Towers Watson.* Retrieved January 18, 2012, from U.S. Tort Cost Trends: 2010 Update: http://www.towerswatson.com/assets/pdf/3424/Towers-Watson-Tort-Report-1.pdf.

Travel India Company. (2006). *Nephrology—Dialysis and Kidney Transplants in India.* Retrieved January 18, 2012, from Medical Tourism in India: http://www.indian-medical-tourism.com/nephrology-india.html.

US Census Bureau. (2011, May). *US Census Bureau.* Retrieved January 18, 2012, from The Hispanic Population: 2010: http://www.census.gov/prod/cen2010/briefs/c2010br-04.pdf.

US Census Bureau. (2012). *Education: Educational Attainment.* Retrieved January 18, 2012, from 2012 Statistical Abstract, National Data Book: http://www.census.gov/compendia/statab/cats/education/educational_attainment.html.

US Census Bureau. (2012). *Income, Expenditures, Poverty, & Wealth.* Retrieved January 18, 2012, from 2012 Statistical Abstract: National Data Book: http://www.census.gov/compendia/statab/cats/income_expenditures_poverty_wealth.html.

United Network for Organ Sharing. (2012). *Estimated US Average 2011 Billed Charges Per Transplant.* Retrieved January 18, 2012, from

Transplant Living: http://www.transplantliving.org/before-the-transplant/financing-a-transplant/the-costs/.

Von Drehle, D. (2012, June 29). Roberts Rules: What the Health Care Decision Means for the Country. Retrieved August 15, 2012, from *Time Magazine*: http://swampland.time.com/2012/06/29/roberts-rules-what-the-health-care-decision-means-for-the-country/#ixzz23eHbXg80.

Walmsley, R. (2009, January). *International Centre for Prison Studies.* Retrieved January 18, 2012, from World Prison Population List (8th ed): http://www.prisonstudies.org/info/downloads/wppl-8th_41.pdf.

World Health Organization. (2010). *Health Systems Financing: The Path to Universal Coverage.* Retrieved July 12, 2012, from World Health Report: http://www.who.int/whr/2010/en/.

www.ingramcontent.com/pod-product-compliance
Lightning Source LLC
Chambersburg PA
CBHW030839180526
45163CB00004B/1388